PRIMITIVE ART

Primitive Art

adapted by Michael Batterberry
and Ariane Ruskin

Foreword by Howard Conant, Ed.D.
New York University

McGRAW-HILL BOOK COMPANY
New York · San Francisco · Toronto

Also in the Discovering Art Series:

CHINESE & ORIENTAL ART, adapted by Michael Batterberry

GREEK & ROMAN ART, adapted by Ariane Ruskin and Michael Batterberry

NINETEENTH CENTURY ART, adapted by Ariane Ruskin

SEVENTEENTH & EIGHTEENTH CENTURY ART, adapted by Ariane Ruskin

TWENTIETH CENTURY ART, by Michael Batterberry

ART OF THE EARLY RENAISSANCE, adapted by Michael Batterberry

ART OF THE HIGH RENAISSANCE, adapted by Ariane Ruskin

PREHISTORIC ART AND ART OF THE ANCIENT NEAR EAST, adapted by Ariane Ruskin

ART OF THE MIDDLE AGES, adapted by Michael Batterberry

Acknowledgment is hereby given to Purnell & Sons, Ltd. for the right to base this work on the text of the magazine series "Discovering Art," and to Fratelli Fabbri Editori for the right to make adaptations from the Italian text of *Capolavori Nei Secoli*.

PRIMITIVE ART
Illustrations copyright © 1961–1964, 1973, by Fratelli Fabbri Editori, Milan, Italy. No part of this work may be reproduced without the permission of the publisher. All Rights Reserved. *Printed in Italy*.

Library of Congress Catalog Card Number: 72-2295

FOREWORD

by Howard Conant

Professor and Chairman, Department of Art Education; and Head, Division of Creative Arts, New York University

THE MYSTICAL AND ritualistic origins of much that remains unknown about art lies unseen before our very eyes in the works illustrated and discussed in this handsome and compelling study of *Primitive Art*. A careful reading of this profoundly insightful text, and a study of the more than 300 full-color illustrations which accompany it will open new vistas to the many readers of this volume. Countless people in preceding generations have also had their curiosity piqued by the challenge of art's hidden secrets. But the innermost meanings, the deepest mystical bases of art forms such as those dealt with in this volume, will continue to lie hidden to all but the artists and tribal cults who created them. The most profound scholars, the ablest writers, the best illustrations, and even the finest museum collections of original works, can do no more than bring us to the edge of the inner core of art's aesthetic essence. We can, nevertheless, peer within and react with better-educated wonderment. In spite of primitive art's inscrutability, it will surprise some readers to learn that of all periods and styles in the entire history of art, that which we call "primitive" is one of the simplest in basic design, the most straightforward—indeed, wholly unabashed —in the subject matter with which it deals. At the same time, it is the least involved with tricks, illusions, and other forms of artifice. The superficial and sophisticated mannerisms of, say, eighteenth century painting, are absent here, as are such artistically unessential techniques as perspective and representational rendering. How magnificently paradoxical, therefore, and how intellectually challenging are confrontations with works of art such as these whose childlike simplicity, artistic naïvete, and technical innocence belie the subdued fervor of their evocative power.

"Primitive art," as the authors explain, is a term given to the arts of people who lived in a simpler state of society than our own. In actuality, the art forms of primitive people often exceed in quality the works of art produced in today's technologically advanced cultures. In pondering this matter, the reader will naturally ask the culturally-essential question of whether or not it is possible to maintain and develop meaningful cultural values in a society such as ours, which places such importance on materialistic gain and technological advancement.

Primitive Art is an excellent source of information for persons interested in better understanding the basic essentials of human social life. By studying the life patterns of primitive people, we can learn much about such presently compelling matters as the conservation of natural resources, product obsolesence, and pollution control. Most important of all, perhaps, may be our realization that the arts were considered by primitive man to be as important as food, clothing, shelter, health, procreation, and even death. Actually, the arts of primitive man were (and still are) such an essential part of everything he did that they lost their identity as individual art forms and blended imperceptibly—beautifully—into his total life style.

5

Like its nine companion volumes in the handsomely illustrated and richly informative *Discovering Art* series, *Primitive Art* should be placed in every school and community library, and will be warmly welcomed in many homes. It has, in addition, high usage potential as a humanities unit text, where it could provide the intellectual depth and subject detail so often lacking in such courses.

CONTENTS

Introduction

OUTSIDE THE great body of art bequeathed to us by the ancient civilizations of the Old World of Europe and the Near East, which forms the heritage of what we call western civilization, there exist many other traditions of art. There is, of course, the great pageant of Oriental art. But others, too, developed in isolation, among the tribes of Africa and Oceania, in remote parts of Asia, and in North and South America. They reflect the spiritual life, the environment, and the technical achievements of peoples living in a simpler state of society than our own, often in a tribal society, and for this reason they are called *primitive* traditions of art. They consist of styles and techniques that developed over many generations, without any contact with the rules imposed on western art. These arts have their own rules, very different from those of the West, although their traditions are often as long, as varied and as rich. Above all, they teach us one impressive lesson: that all men, at all times, have had their art, and that the desire for what we call "artistic expression," the desire to represent life as it is in an artistic way and to beautify it, must be common to all men, and a part of human nature itself.

Eskimo Art and the Art of the North American Indian

THE SPECIES WE CALL modern man did not spring into existence in the western hemisphere. He is, in fact, a relative newcomer to the forests and deserts of North and South America. It was not until perhaps thirty thousand years ago that nomadic peoples began to migrate from the plains of Asia to the American continents, probably by way of Siberia, the Bering Strait, and Alaska. Gradually these peoples came to inhabit almost all of the two continents, and each group developed a culture of its own, adapted to the terrain of the region—forest or plain, hot or cold—in which it lived. Each developed, too, its own art.

From the very earliest times, from the time of the Ice Age itself, which held Europe in its grip until ten thousand years before Christ, arctic hunters have lived in the frozen regions within sight of the retreating ice cap, hunting the seal and walrus with weapons of bone. They have always lived much the same life, not only in Alaska and the western hemisphere, but throughout the entire Arctic Circle, where they wandered freely—in Greenland, northern Scandinavia, and Siberia. Their customs varied as little from place to place as from period to period. The Eskimos of Alaska, northern Canada, and Greenland are the largest and most familiar race of these arctic hunters, and their customs, still alive today, reflect the life of man in a cold climate from time immemorial.

For most of the Eskimos, during the greater part of the year, the vast desert of ice and the icy sea itself are the only visible landscape. In spring and summer the huge expanse of the tundra reveals itself, giving the Eskimo his only glimpse of nature's softer loveliness. "We can see from the tracks how the Arctic hare has leaped about by the bare patches, and nibbled at the young shoots. Ground squirrels and lemmings emerge from their burrows in the sandy slopes and sniff at all this shimmering light. Flocks of rock ptarmigan and willow grouse flap with their heavy wings over the snow and settle, twenty, fifty, a hundred together, and fill the air with their calling. Caribou tracks are everywhere. . . . When [they] are to windward it is sometimes possible to get quite close to them. Small herds can always be seen in the distance. In an endless, multilegged row their dark forms stand out on the ridge against the clear sky."

But ice, snow, and sea are the typical environment of the Eskimos and govern their existence. The first problem, of finding somewhere to live, is solved in most cases with snow. An area is selected where the snow is sufficiently hard and of exactly the right consistency; then large blocks are cut with a whalebone or antler knife, and placed together in an ascending spiral, the dug-out hollow in the snow remaining to form the sunken floor of the house. Each block is trimmed to fit the previous one, and is pushed into place with a vigorous blow of the fist. The blocks are placed to incline more and more inwards, forming a dome which is then finally perfected by blocking up the joints. The whole process would take no more than an hour or so. Inside, a seat of snow is made to run round the sides, with a larger platform at the rear to serve as both table and bed. It is covered with mats of heather twigs, then with skins of caribou, bear, or musk-ox. A window may be formed with a block of clear ice. This type of hut has been replaced in many areas by other types, and in Alaska, where there are quantities of driftwood and timber, houses are built entirely of timber and covered outside with sod and earth.

In many areas, where there is no wood or heather for fires, the lamp is the center of Eskimo domestic life, serving as both heat and light. It has a half-moon-shaped bowl, cut from soapstone, in which the blubber is placed, with a wick of moss along the front edge. It burns night and day, with a soft light, and if properly attended never smokes. In some cases, a soapstone cooking-pot for meat would hang over the lamp.

Getting through the winter is the Eskimo's greatest challenge, and he is dependent on hunting for success. Among tribes that move at frequent intervals to new sites and have no permanent winter houses, the dog sledge is all important. Once the hunting ground is reached, the essential weapon is the harpoon, a loose head of tusk with a blade fastened to a short line of seal thong held in the hand. The blade today is iron, but formerly was stone or bone. In summer, when seals come up onto the ice and bask in the sun, the hunter clothes himself in sealskin and creeps up on the animal, imitating its antics until he is close enough to use the harpoon.

In contrast to the ingenuity and skill of hunting methods, the organization of Eskimo society tends to be extremely primitive. There is neither class, rank, nor state, though generally in each settlement one man is tacitly accepted as the leader. Hunting and trapping grounds are common property, and large catches, such as whales, are communally shared. (Personal property is respected, however, and thieving is practically unknown.) Similarly, though marriage is a natural state, and Eskimos are devoted to their children, the exchange of wives is common, for both formal and practical reasons. Thus when a man is going on a journey and his own wife cannot accompany him, he may make a temporary exchange with a friend.

The monotony of long winter nights and bad weather is lightened by various recreations. The most spectacular are the drum dances, held far into the night in both winter and summer. The dancers' movement is heavy; they bend their knees, lean the body forward at the same time, and sway. Then there are numerous unwritten legends—the most important part of the cultural heritage—which glorify the historic achievements of ancestors and have an edifying effect upon the children. More personal, more poignant, are the songs. Each man has his own, and the sole right to sing it; and the poetry which many of them contain is perhaps the closest one approaches to the yearnings of these frost-bound people. As an ancient West Greenlander once sang:

O warmth of summer sweeping over the
land!
Not a breath of wind,
Not a cloud,
And among the mountains
The grazing caribou,
The dear caribou,
In the blue distance.
O how entrancing,
O how joyful,
I lay me on the ground, sobbing. . . .

Most important, the Eskimo triumph over the monotony and hardships of long dark winters and extreme cold enabled them to use their imaginative powers to beautify the objects with which they lived. Eskimo art has, in fact, a long history. Two thousand years ago the Eskimos of

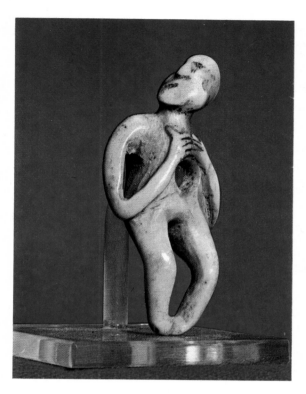

I-1. Bone arrow straightener

I-2. Bone female figurines

what was called the Bering Sea culture were decorating their implements with scroll-like patterns and figures like the eye of an animal. Soon there were charming animal figures carved in bone and freehand engravings on ivory of outdoor and domestic scenes.

Above all, the Eskimo artists, who spent the long winter nights fashioning decorative objects by the light of a whale-fat lamp, were fascinated by the natural forms of life of which they saw so little and which were so precious to them. They portrayed man and the animals of the wilderness again and again, often skillfully modeling objects into human or animal form. The strangely twisted figure in Plate I-1 is in fact an arrow straightener made of bone. The hole in the center of the figure is used to level sticks when they are being straightened for use as arrows. The bone female figures in Plate I-2 were probably used as amulets. Jewelry,

harpoons, fishhooks, knives, and pipes were all elaborately carved. We must remember that the Eskimo artist was limited to working small pieces of bone, ivory, or driftwood with very primitive tools, and this is why the treatment of the figures seems simplified. Still they are vigorous and lively and finely finished.

Fur, feathers, or braided fiber might be added to an artistic object for decoration. The artist was a hunter like his fellows, but known to be skilled in the decorations he created in his spare time. Such "works of art" were never made to be sold, but to be used by the family, or given as gifts, especially at the time of winter festivals, when the members of many villages would assemble to exchange presents, attend religious ceremonies, arrange marriages, and enjoy themselves generally.

The scenes of Eskimo life we see painted on a fragment from a boat in Plate I-3 and etched on walrus tusk pipe in Plate I-4 are equally lively. On the boat fragment we see choppy, shark-infested waters, dry land and the deeply pitched roof of a wooden Eskimo house, along with trees and little human figures—the entire Eskimo world, in fact. Eskimo boats, or *kayaks,* were painted with such scenes for magical purposes. A woman might draw these pictures, but only men painted them, using mineral colors mixed with blood and urine and applied with squirrel-hair brushes. Above all, the telling of a story was most important.

Although the human beings on the walrus pipe are only stick figures, they go through the motions of pulling sledges, hewing wood, cooking over a fire, and dancing with such easy, natural movement that they seem almost realistic. There are many such engravings on walrus ivory with incised lines filled with soot or red ocher. The little figures going about their easily recognizable activities almost amount to a kind of pictorial writing. Most of these engraved objects, bows or tobacco pipes, date from the eighteenth and nineteenth

I-3. Painted wooden fragment from a boat

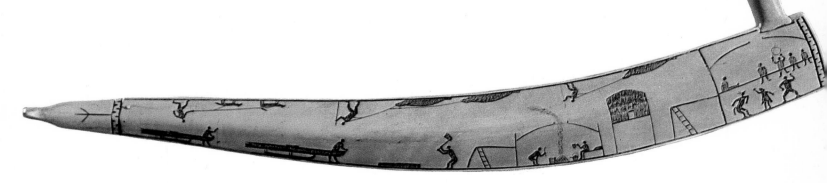

I-4. Walrus tusk tobacco pipe

centuries. Again we see the whole of Eskimo life in one small space. It is as if men, constricted in their daily toils, could step aside and observe themselves and refuse to be constricted in spirit.

Eskimo religion is of a simple type, rather like that of North American Indians in general, in which nature is seen as inhabited by friendly or hostile spirits, or *inva.* Such a form of belief—that objects have spirits of their own—is called *animism.* The *medicine man,* or priest, of Eskimo society was the *shaman.* Shamans were "supernaturally" chosen men who could fight hostile spirits, detect culprits, and go into trance-like states when it was believed that the spirit took possession of the body. In Alaska especially shamans frequently beat drums and wore masks, and these were important elements of the great dance feasts, which were intended to express the experiences of the shaman in the land of the spirits. The Eskimos lavished on these drums and masks their greatest artistry. In Plate I-5 we see the decoration of a shaman's drum from Lapland, the arctic region of Scandinavia. Such drums were often painted with historical scenes, represented by little pictographs which, drawn with a firm and decorative hand, tell of events in the lives of the tribe's ancestors—hunting stories full of magic. Often these events were dramatized to the beating of drums on which they were depicted. Here the figures have a less human appearance than those on the walrus pipe. They are more stylized or conventional, representing the human figure in an established way recognizable to those who painted it. Yet great attention has been given to the abstract design of the decoration, and like the pipe it suggests a lively interest in events.

The use of masks in Eskimo ritual dances was based on what is called sympathetic

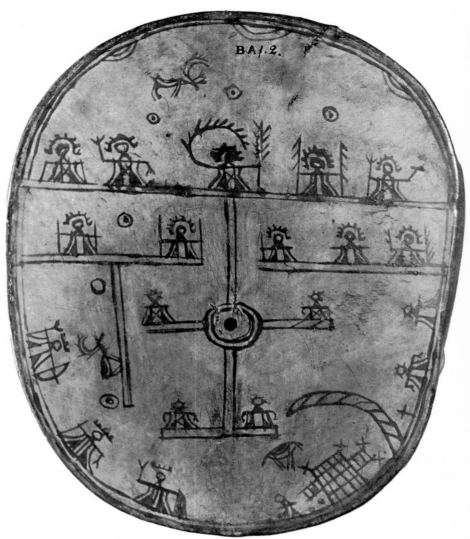

I-5. A shaman's drum

magic. Primitive peoples in all times, and that includes the peoples of prehistoric Europe, have often believed that the spirit of a creature could be invoked by its artistic representation and that what is done to the image of an animal (or man, for that matter) will affect the animal or man himself. Before the hunt the cave dwellers of the Old Stone Age painted on the walls of their caves pictures of buffalo, wild boars, and such, often shot full of arrows. These pictures were intended to give the hunter power over his prey.

So it was that the Eskimos felt that a dance in which the shaman imitated a cer-

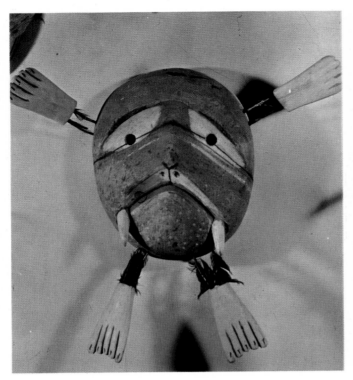

I-6. Wooden mask

I-7. Bone mask

tain animal would invoke the spirit of that species of animal and make droves of them available to the hunter. The Eskimos wished to remain on friendly terms with the animals they hunted. They hoped to achieve this by performing ceremonies and dances in honor of the spirit of the animals in question. They also restored those killed to life by returning the animal's bladder (thought to be the seat of the soul) to the sea. They felt that the seal or bear, assured of a second life, would welcome the hunter's harpoon or arrow.

Apart from masks of animal spirits, the Eskimos also created masks for the shaman's assistants and caricatures of members of the tribe as masks for actors in comic dramas. Oddly enough, it is sometimes difficult to tell animal masks from human ones, as the animal's spirit is often thought to have a human face. Other masks represent only the animal appearance and still others com-

bine animal and human characteristics. In the earliest periods these masks were carved from large pieces of whalebone; later they were sometimes built up from smaller pieces of bone, and sometimes made of driftwood. They often have elaborate appendages, at times simplified into one shield-like structure, identifying the being represented.

In Plate I-6 we see a mask that, without appendages, is a simple representation of a human face. In Plates I-7 and I-8 the human face is transformed into the visages of forceful and terrifying spiritual creatures. In Plate I-9 the mask and the shield around it are converted into one brilliant abstract pattern. In creating these, the many faces of nature, the Eskimos have been endlessly imaginative. It is particularly extraordinary that they were able to achieve so many effects when they had so little material with which to work—some ivory, some wood, and a few colors—red, white, blue, and sometimes green. The artist is aiming, not at an exact representation of man or animal, but at expressing some overpowering emotion at the heart of nature, and in this he has succeeded amazingly well.

Why did the Eskimo peoples of Alaska never move to the more comfortable climates farther south? It may be that, once accustomed to hunting and fishing in the Far North, they did not wish to learn new habits. It might also be that they were prevented by the many tribes of Indians who inhabited what is now Canada and the United States, hunting and fishing in the immensely rich forests and rivers of the body of the North American continent.

Among these Indians there were as many different ways of life as there were tribes and as many different styles of art. Still the tribes of certain large areas, living under similar conditions, as, for example, the Indians of the eastern coastal forests, or the Indians of the central North American plains, had much in common.

Like the Eskimo, the Indian tribes of North America have had a long history, but unfortunately an unrecorded one, and so the exploits of the many tribes that roamed the continent before the arrival of the first settlers remain part of the unknown. Recent archeology, however, has helped us to learn much of life of the Indians before Columbus and even of peoples whose very existence was once undreamed.

I-9. Wooden mask

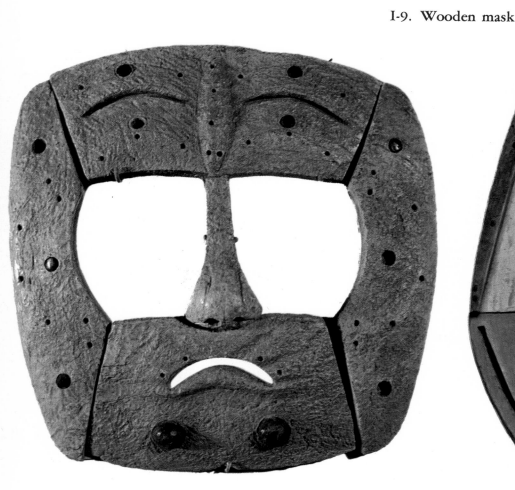

I-8. Bone mask

For example, about a thousand years ago, a remarkable civilization spread from the Gulf Coast up the Mississippi valley. The people farmed extensively and depended on their crops for a livelihood, though hunting and fishing were also good. They lived in houses of wattle and thatch over poles, in semipermanent villages or towns. Like the Aztecs and the Mayas of Mexico, the people built mounds for their civic and religious centers, but more crudely; the mounds were of rubble, topped with earth, and the buildings on top, of wood and thatch. The largest is the Emerald Mound in Mississippi, which is thirty-five feet high and seven acres in extent, with six smaller mounds on top. In the North, effigy mounds developed, in the shape of birds or animals, often on the top of other mounds; for example, the great Serpent Mound in Ohio. The construction of these mounds, without machinery, argues long periods of leisure from earning a livelihood, which perhaps also explains how the Mound Builders developed some of their art, especially in their modeling and carving.

In Plates I-10, I-11, and I-12 we see what are called earthenware effigy vases. These jars take the form of little crouching figures, and although exactly what purpose they served is unknown, they seem to have some connection with death. These little forms are well modeled, and although not strictly realistic, like the masks of the Eskimos, they suggest powerful emotions powerfully—in this case, a strange kind of dread. They are also decorative and pleasing to the eye. As we shall see later, they very much resemble the works of the Indians of ancient Mexico—a most intriguing fact.

The Mound Builders of the Mississippi have no part in our traditional notion of the American Indian. Much of their civilization lay many centuries buried when Columbus saw land. The first peoples with whom the earliest settlers came in contact were the Indians of the eastern woodlands.

When English and French settlers landed on the New England coast, they found a country covered with birch forests, inhabited by scattered tribes living in wigwams. These were made by covering frames of bent poles with birch bark, rushes, or woven mats. The Indians there practiced a little agriculture, and hunted the abundant game. They taught the white settlers to plant corn, bake clams, make canoes, and to use seaweed as a fertilizer, to eat pumpkins, and smoke tobacco.

But the hard struggle for existence, combined with warfare against neighboring tribes, left the Indians of the eastern seaboard little time for the cultivation of the arts. They covered birch bark—which they used for most of their possessions—with carved designs or drawings in pictographs, which took the place of writing. They also ornamented the bark with a curious double-curved design, and decorated their clothing, generally made of skins, with porcupine quills dyed and sewn closely together in a pattern resembling a textile. Sculpture was not developed although the Iroquois of New York State skillfully fashioned masks, to be worn by members of their False Face society at ceremonies to frighten away the evil spirits of disease.

One remarkable craft of the Indians of the eastern woodlands, however, was the making of *wampum* beads. A longish strip of clam shell, or some other thick shell, would be sanded down to a cylinder shape; then a hole would be bored through the length of the cylinder. To bore the hole, with a stone or wooden drill, amounted to a very fine art. As only a tiny part of a clam shell is purple, and the rest white,

I-10. Earthenware effigy vase

I-12. Painted earthenware effigy vase

I-11. Earthenware effigy vase

17

purple wampum beads became very valuable. They were bought for high prices by inland tribes, and even colonists used them for currency. With the advent of European trade, the Indians began to use imported foreign beads, which they sewed on to belts, bags, and such in intricate and usually abstract patterns. Moreover, their own wampum beads were copied in porcelain in Europe and traded to them.

It was not the Indians of the eastern forests, but the Indians of the Great Plains, extending from the Mississippi River to the Rocky Mountains and from the Gulf of Mexico into Canada, who have created the popular concept of the American Indian, a warrior clad in skins and feathers galloping over the prairies. No such figure, however, was to be seen before 1700.

At least two centuries before that a culture had become established on the thinly populated plains, among the people of the Sioux, the Comanche, and the Cheyenne. They lived in skin tents, called *tepees,* used dogs as beasts of burden, and hunted the numerous wild buffalo with stone arrows, a remarkable skill. But their whole way of life changed after they captured some horses which had escaped from a Spanish expedition under de Soto in 1538. Other horses, brought by the Spanish to New Mexico, ran wild and spread east, and their numbers increased on the plains. The Indians could now move from place to place as the horses could carry all the belongings and also drag the poles and heavy hides necessary to make their tepees. When the buffalo were in their territory they lived richly and had the leisure to cultivate their crafts.

These Indians decorated everything they possessed. The men painted the skin tepees and blankets with little naturalistic representations of men and animals, while the women painted straight linear designs on the deerskin clothing and *parfleches* (skin bags for storing meat). The women also practiced a lavish dyed porcupine-quill embroidery (similar to that of the east woodlands Indians) with which they decorated tobacco pouches, bags, knife sheaths, and some of their clothing in geometric designs. Their skill in rich beadwork, which replaced quillwork after European beads became available, was responsible, later, for what we think of as the handsome, typical Indian mode of dress. But European traders could not sell beads of any color to the Indians. They had excellent if reserved taste, preferring, for example, white patterns on light blue to more garish combinations, which they occasionally created for sale to the settlers. And as ever, they preferred simple geometric designs featuring stripes, bars, squares, circles, and triangles, although adaptations of European designs were later attempted.

Both the eastern forest Indians and the Indians of the Great Plains found their greatest artistic expression in dances, songs, and ceremonies. All in all, they gave little thought to what we generally call the visual arts—painting and large sculpture. Moreover, they had no architecture to speak of. Houses were built for the purpose of habitation with little regard to design. But important art was produced by the Indian tribes of North America who will seem less familiar—the tribes of the Northwest, the Pacific coastal regions from Alaska to Oregon, and the tribes of the Southwest, especially the Pueblo Indians of the region of New Mexico.

A rocky, indented coastline stretches northwards from the mouth of the Columbia River in Oregon to the shores of southern Alaska. It is bounded by a sea, where salmon are plentiful, and its shores are flanked with great forests of cedar trees. But this area is cut off from the rest of the continent by the Rocky Mountains, and its peoples, although the sea and many rivers afforded them easy communication with each other, were cut off from those of the rest of North America.

The Indians who lived along this coast, the Tlingit, Haida, Kwakiutl, Chinook, and others, won an easy livelihood from the sea, and the cedars surrounding them provided wood for houses and canoes. The forest also gave them wood for their furnishings, their mats, eating vessels, clubs, fishhooks, spoons, rattles, masks, and armor. The chief occupation of the men, when not fishing, was making these tools and decorating them, concentrating in the ornament the power of their mythology and something common to all men, the aggressive pursuit of social prestige.

Society was divided into chiefs, freemen, and slaves (captured in war or taken from other tribes) and these were divided into clans, composed of several family groups. Social prestige was gained not only from the ancestry of the clan—its names, songs, myths, and dances, handed down from one generation to another—but also from the possession of rich and beautiful objects.

One of the most important ways of asserting social prestige was the giving of a *potlatch* (the word is an Indian one meaning "gift"), a ceremonial feast. These would be given by a chief for such occasions as a marriage, or the birth of a son, but more particularly in order to establish his claim to a new name, a new chieftainship, or some prerogative on behalf of his children. At these feasts he would demonstrate his wealth by bestowing gifts on his guests; blankets like the one in Plate I-13 cunningly woven of cedar bark and the wool of the mountain goat into elaborate

geometric and symbolic patterns; richly carved and inlaid bowls and masks; or large copper shields etched with a design or family crest, in practice useless, but sometimes worth to the owner as much as ten thousand blankets. The recipients were bound to return gifts of as great value, with interest, or, if the host burned his possessions in public, to burn their own. This could be a way of bankrupting or shaming social rivals. This striving for prestige, in a society where a rich food supply and slaves provided much leisure, was a perfect background for the development of art.

I-13. Chilkat blanket

The prestige of a clan, and also a great deal of artistic inspiration, was expressed in the *totem pole*. These totem poles, tall cedar columns, ten to seventy feet in height, were erected at the doors of the large, pitched-roof wooden structures that often housed the whole clan, or stood as memorials to the dead. The poles traced in elaborate carvings of intertwined beasts and men, one above the other, the heraldic insignia of the clan and glorious episodes, real or imaginary, of the life of the owner or his ancestors. They are among the most monumental wood carvings ever created by man.

The sculpture we find in the totem poles probably developed most during the last two hundred years, since the Indians were able to obtain steel tools from the Europeans. Before this time, poles, cut with stone axes, seem to have been smaller and fewer in number. In the early poles, too, only the details were painted in black, red, white, and blue-green. Later poles were painted all over. The styles in which they were carved came to follow extremely conventionalized forms. Figures, often representing spirits (Plate I-14) rather than resembling anything in nature, have been simplified into an almost geometric pattern. As we have seen in their blankets, the Indians of the Northwest liked to cover objects with an ornamental linear design covering as much of the surface as possible, and leaving little rest for the eye, and this was true of their treatment of totem poles as well.

As with their northern neighbors the Eskimos, the Indians of the Northwest found their chief artistic inspiration in the animals with which they lived. *Totemism* is a belief that a man is closely related in a particular way to a certain animal or mythological being. Thus a familiar animal, such as the eagle, raven, wolf, or

I-14. Engraved wooden plaque

whale, would be sacred to a certain clan, and would appear on its totem poles and in its masks and sculpture. The clans would often not only use an animal as an insignia but adopt the animal name as a clan name, and in the North the highest-ranking families would trace their descent back to one of these supernatural animals, or to a human who had had some experience with a supernatural being and received special powers from it. These might be, for example, the right to dance certain dances, sing particular songs, own certain salmon areas, and hunt whales. Above all, totem animals were not killed. Like the animals whom the Eskimos "restored to life," they were to be appeased.

The legend of the origin of the Bear clan told that a woman was captured and married by the king of the Bears, to whom she bore a child half-human, half-bear. She was eventually rescued by a group of hunters. The ancestor of the Eagle clan was a being who came to earth in the form of an eagle, and turned himself into a human being, except for the nose, which remained a beak.

The raven, a common sight on the Northwest coast, was regarded as the creator of all things and benefactor of man. The legend ran that before the earth was endowed with light, the people asked Raven to acquire it for them from the house of the supernatural being, where it was kept. Raven flew to the house of the supernatural, and after waiting hidden for a few days, seized his opportunity when the daughter of the supernatural went to a stream for a cup of water. He changed into an evergreen needle and floated into the cup. But the girl was suspicious and removed the needle before drinking. The following day Raven floated into her cup in the form of a grain of sand, so tiny that it escaped her notice and she drank it with the water. As a result, the girl soon afterward gave birth to a child which was Raven in disguise. He grew rapidly and soon began to cry for the sun, which was kept in a box in the corner. He persisted until the supernatural being allowed him to play with it, but every night it was returned to its box.

One night, when the supernaturals were asleep, Raven assumed his original form, took the sun from the box, and tried to escape through the smoke hole in the roof. The grandfather was awakened at this point by the sudden light and called to the flames of the fire to catch the bird. As the flames leaped upwards, the smoke turned Raven black, but he managed to break free, and flew toward the earth. The grandfather followed in such close pursuit that Raven, to make the sun easier to carry, broke pieces of it off and threw them into the sky, where they became stars. But the supernatural continued to gain on him, and Raven was

obliged to throw a larger piece away, which became the moon. Finally, in fear of being caught, Raven threw the remaining piece into the sky, and this became the sun. Raven now returned to earth, and thus he became black, and the people on earth acquired the sun, moon, and stars.

Such mythology was based on animals or on supernatural beings who changed their shape at will. The reverence of the Northwest Indians for these figures was given religious expression in ceremonies, lasting three days or more, conducted by secret societies during the winter months. These were under the direction of shamans like those of the Eskimos. All who took part in the ceremonies, singers and dancers, wore elaborate costumes and masks, and were supposedly possessed by the powers they represented.

If we compare the mask of an old woman (Plate I-15) with a mask representing a spirit (Plate I-16), we will see that like those of the Eskimos, these masks might vary in style from complete naturalism to a representation of the human face that is almost completely abstract, depending on the use to which they were to be put. The mask of an old woman is a masterpiece of closely observed realism by any standard. The straggly hair, thin bloodless lips, deep wrinkles, and missing teeth all suggest old age as powerfully as it has ever been displayed in art. And we can see that the Indians of the Northwest could portray the anatomy of the human face with as much sensitivity and realism as they chose. But they often preferred a more abstract and more powerful portrayal for the sometimes terrifying spirits of their beliefs. The black mask surmounted by a crown of leather strips in Plate I-17 could only fill the observer with fear. It is a human face become by distortion and exaggeration—its dark

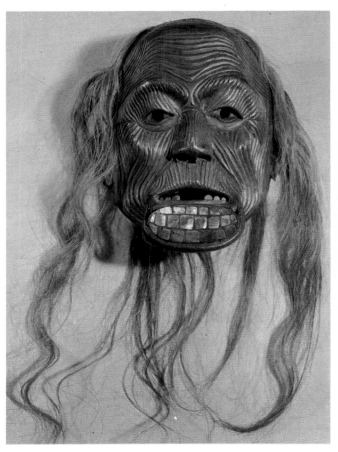

I-15. Wooden mask of an old woman

I-16. Mask representing a spirit

color, glaring eyes, and bared teeth—a face of horror. The copper mask in Plate I-18 is meant to represent the mosquito, and its sinister face, surrounded by wings and surmounted by a stinger nose, suggests the insect perfectly. A great deal of symbolism was used in such carvings; a trapezoid shape represented the killer whale, for example, and hands, eyes, and other shapes were used for purely decorative purposes.

The mask in Plate I-19 presents a colorful abstract pattern. On either side of it we see movable additions representing marine monsters. Particularly ingenious mechanical masks were made by the Indians of the Northwest. Eyes were made to roll and jaws to chomp by pulling strings. Others were constructed with appendages that could be made to flap by the same means, and occasionally the whole front of a mask could be made to open, revealing a different face below. Others were enhanced by huge bird beaks, or the six-foot-long body of a killer whale, complete with movable flippers and tail. These would be painted in brilliant shades—red, yellow, and brown ocher, blue-green, black, and white—composed of powdered pigments mixed with chewed salmon eggs and applied with fiber or bristle brushes.

The ceremonies were often held in the huge houses, lit by crackling fires with smoke and sparks vanishing through the smoke hole into the night. It was in such a setting that these monstrous apparitions appeared; the dancers were aided in creating

I-17. Wooden mask

I-18. Copper mask representing a mosquito

magic and mystery by their sleight of hand, using stringed puppets, false-bottomed chests, and bags filled with blood held in their mouths and bitten at suitable dramatic moments. The effect must have been staggering.

In small carvings such as pipe bowls or little figurines the Indians of the Northwest used whale or walrus ivory. Among the most interesting objects made of this material were "soul traps" used by the shaman to cure diseases. These were hollow tubes with open ends carved to represent jaws and in the middle a small human figure, often inlaid with haliotis shell. It was believed that illness was a sign that the sufferer's soul had escaped from his body and had to be caught and returned to him by means of the soul trap before he would recover. The curious ivory carving in Plate I-20 may have been such a soul trap. In its contorted form we can see, to the right, the head of a bird of prey; in the middle, two foetus-like figures, probably spirits; and to the left, a large eye with trapezoidal projection signifying the killer whale. In Plate I-21 we see a bone carving of a man and a spirit (his animal counterpart) that suggests on a small scale the figures of a totem pole. The individual details of the elaborately intertwined figures in such delicate and intricate carvings of the Northwest are fascinating and demand our close attention.

When we speak of the Indians of the Southwest we mean those who live between the Great Plains and the west coast, in New

I-19. Mask with movable appendages

Mexico, Arizona, Utah, Nevada, and California. Among the tribes, the Zuñi, Hopi, Apache, Navaho, and others, that inhabit the deserts and high plateaus of the region, we find perhaps the most fascinating of all North American Indian cultures.

The Indians of the Southwest had developed a unique way of life by 500 A.D. They were mostly agricultural peoples, for whom the growing of crops was more important than hunting. Many lived in villages, called *pueblos,* consisting of stone houses—great communal buildings of one-room dwellings arranged side by side and in terraces, like modern apartment houses, (Plate I-21a). One such building, Pueblo Bonito, was 667 feet long and 315 feet wide. These structures were geometric in form and plastered with adobe (dried mud), presenting a strange appearance, the smooth surface of their walls punctuated here and there by the dark square shadow of a window. Designed for defense against no-

I-20. Ivory carving, probably used as a soul trap

I-21. Bone carving of a man and a spirit

I-21a. Taos Pueblo

madic Indians, the pueblos often had no ground-floor doors, but ladders to the stories above. The ladders could be pulled up in times of danger.

Each village also had one or more *kivas,* rooms that were often underground, entered through a hole in the roof, which were used as men's lounging places, as council rooms, and for religious ceremonies. The interior walls of these chambers might be decorated with paintings executed on the adobe plaster walls in shades of red, yellow, and white, usually in the abstract geometric patterns that give the art of the Pueblo Indians its character.

For individual ceremonies, the Navaho, who did not live in pueblos, created pictures in colored sand on the ground. It was said that the gods had made pictures in black clouds spread on the floor, and in imitation of these, sand pictures were made for ceremonies of healing. For each malady there was a specific chant and design, and after lengthy preparation, the patient was cured by coming in contact with a sand picture on which he was made to sit. These pictures were created in sands of red, yellow, white, and gray-blue, ground from

I-22. Mask of a Katchina

I-24. Mask of the god Tlasiskwa

I-23. Mask of the god Nahatescho

sandstone with the addition of cornmeal, ground flowers, pollen, and parts of plants. The artists were especially trained young men. As it was felt that the sands of these splendid, complex geometric patterns absorbed the disease, they were gathered up after the ceremony and taken far away.

Almost all Pueblo Indians followed the Katchina cult. Katchinas were divine beings who mediated between men and the gods, and who were with them for but half the year. During the summer they were believed to live high in the mountains. In Pueblo ceremonies, the Katchinas were represented by initiated men who wore masks to enact solemn ritual dances. These masks were covered in symbols expressing the elements over which the Katchinas had power—rain, crops, fertility, and such. In

I-25. Katchina dolls

Plates I-22, I-23, and I-24 we see three Katchina masks, from the Zuñi culture. Basically they are painted leather (and sometimes wooden) helmets with slits for eyes, and are decorated by the addition of fur collars or spruce wreaths around the neck, hair, beards, feathers, or other appendages. But one glance will tell us that these masks are very different from those of the Eskimos or the Indians of the Northwest coast. Rather than obvious figures of terror or power we see simple head shapes covered with abstract geometric designs—the clear, clean-cut, and superbly balanced formal designs of which the

Pueblo Indians were so fond. Some of the spirits were friendly, others hostile, but what was of importance to the Pueblo Indians was above all the formal decorative elegance of strict design. These masks were "given life." In a special ceremony a priest rubbed the mask with chewed seeds of corn, squash, and other plants, and after the prescribed blessing, it became "valuable and a person," to be appeased by prayers and regular offerings.

Among the most charming objects in all of Indian art are the Katchina dolls (Plate I-25). These dolls, about one foot high, were made every year to represent the

I-26. Pottery of the Southwest Indians
A. Vase from the Mesa Verde   B. Pottery
bowl

I-27. Pottery of the Southwest Indians   A. Pottery canteen   B. Seed bowl   C. Olla (storage bowl)

dancers in the Katchina ceremonies, masks and all. Sometimes they wear painted clothing and sometimes costumes of real cloth, and all the paraphernalia of the ceremony is repeated in miniature. When the ceremony was over, these colorful little objects were given to the children to instruct them in religion.

There seems to have been a strange reversal of the usual roles among the Pueblo Indians. When not farming or hunting, the men embroidered and made jewelry of turquoise, shell, and brightly colored stone which, during the last century and a half, have been set in silver. The women, on the other hand, did much of the building, and all the plastering of the houses with adobe. They also did fine basketwork and made pottery.

The pottery of the Pueblos shows a development that goes far back into the past. Even the earliest pottery came in hundreds of varieties, dating from perhaps 300 A.D. The designs relied almost entirely on

hatched and solid geometrical shapes in black and white. Vase A in Plate I-26 dates from 1300 A.D. Here we see a design in dark pigment on a white "slip" or wash. Such patterns persisted as a tradition, even when other colors and animal designs, such as we see in vase B, came to be used.

Plate I-27 shows us three examples of traditional shapes of vessels which have been used with only minor variations for generations. Each pueblo tended to specialize in certain decorative patterns and shapes, and it is amazing that these could have been created by people who knew nothing of the potter's wheel, and fired their ware in temporary ovens. The decorations, painted with a firm, free hand and without preconceived patterns, kept to certain basic motifs, and yet new variations were developed almost every year. As ever with the Pueblos, these were bold geometric patterns, often painted in red and black on white: squares, spirals, and sunburst designs precisely drawn. Occasionally, as in Plate I-28, little stylized, almost abstract animal forms would find their way into the design. Above all, the Pueblo potters liked a clean line. They wanted to avoid the "dirty" effect of busy or messy designs. And whether abstract or not, their patterns were always full of bright, lively motion.

North American Indian art is far from dead. The long traditions of Eskimo art, which have remained almost unchanged through the ages, are blossoming today, fostered by the encouragement of art lovers and the Canadian and United States governments, and aided by more modern equipment. The same is true elsewhere. Pueblo women still take pride in the distinctive design of their pottery, and Chilkat blankets of the Northwest are still made in the traditional manner. During the last

two hundred years European motifs have crept in. East coast Indians work floral designs into their beadwork, and Saint Paul has found his way into a totem pole. It is strange, but although much of the religion and social organization of the Eskimos and North American Indians is disappearing, their taste for good design and their genius for the expression of the elemental forces of nature have remained unchanged, and are appreciated by art lovers of the European tradition more than ever before.

I-28. Painted pottery vase

WHEN, in August of 1519, Hernando Cortez and some four hundred wounded and bedraggled Spaniards walked into the city of Mexico and met its ruler, Montezuma, they beheld a civilization as splendid as any they had left behind in Europe, or anything they could have imagined. They found themselves in a city of some 60,000 buildings housing over 300,000 people—a great metropolis of huge plazas kept immaculate by a thousand street cleaners. So highly polished was the pavement of the courtyard of its greatest temple that Cortez's horses could hardly walk on it, and within this courtyard stood a pyramid three hundred feet high. It was a city of gracious houses built around with porticoed courtyards, and in the palaces, the rooms were of porphyry and alabaster, finished with rare woods. Above all, it was a city of gardens. One great fifteenth-century ruler had loved flowers, and built a huge botanical garden with plants from all over Mexico. The palace of King Nezahualcoyotl of Texcoco comprised some three hundred rooms. The rest, the Spaniards tell us, was given over to gardens:

With many fountains, ponds and canals, many fish and birds, and the whole planted with more than two thousand pines . . . and there were several mazes, according to where the king bathed; and once a man was in he could not find the way out . . . and farther on, besides the temples, there was the bird-house, where the king kept all the kinds and varieties of birds, animals, reptiles, and serpents . . . and those which were not to be had

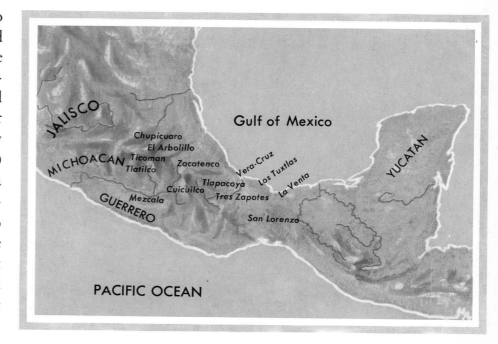

II-1. Map of the area of the early cultures of Mexico, including the Olmec

were represented in gold and precious stones. And the water intended for the fountains, pools and channels for watering the flowers and the trees in this park came from its spring: to bring it it had been necessary to build strong, high, cemented walls of unbelievable size, going from one mountain to another with an aqueduct on top which came out at the highest part of the park.

Moreover, Montezuma's capital, Tenochtitlán (on the site of modern Mexico City), was a cosmopolitan metropolis—the religious and administrative center of an empire and a vast marketplace. The Spaniards compared it to Venice, Rome, and Madrid. Bernal Díaz, a follower of Cortez, described all that he saw in detail, and of market day he said:

Every kind of merchandise was kept separate and had its fixed place marked for it. There were the dealers in gold, silver and precious stones, feathers, cloaks and embroidered goods and male and female slaves . . . there were those who sold woven cloth, and chocolate merchants . . . those who sold ropes and the sandals they wore on their feet . . . and in another part were skins of tigers and lions, otters, jackals and deer, badgers, mountain cats and other wild animals, some tanned and some untanned. There were sellers of kidney beans and sage, and other vegetables and herbs in another place and in yet another they were selling fowls, birds with great dewlaps [turkeys], rabbits . . . there were the women selling cooked food, flour and honey cake and tripe, there was cochineal, tobacco . . . there were the sellers of pitch pine for torches and other things of that kind. . . . But why waste so many words on the goods in their great market? They have a building there also in which three judges sit and there are officials like constables who examine the merchandise. . . .

For currency in their larger transactions the Aztecs used quills of gold dust.

With all the wealth of merchandise, those who were permitted to do so by their rank or their calling could appear as resplendent as art could make them. The women used mirrors made of carefully polished obsidian and pyrites, and ointments, creams, and scent. The courtesan, the companion of the young unmarried warriors, "grooms herself and dresses with such care that when she is thoroughly ready she looks like a flower. And to make herself ready she first looks in her glass, she bathes, washes and freshens herself in order to

please. She makes up her face with a yellow cream called axin, which gives her a dazzling complexion; and sometimes, being a loose, lost woman, she puts on rouge. She has also the habit of dyeing her teeth red with cochineal and of wearing her hair loose for more beauty . . . she perfumes herself with an odoriferous censer, and in walking about she chews tzictli, making a clacking noise with her teeth like castanets."

Clothes and footwear were relatively plain but nobles, according to their rank, could wear dazzlingly colored headdresses, bronze-green plumes of quetzal feathers, immense butterflies, cloth or feather mosaic banners or decorated shields. Before the crowds on the central square, the emperor would appear, rigid beneath the gold and turquoise diadem, amidst the brilliance of green plumes, while the armor, the emblems, and the banners of the great men formed a mosaic of a thousand colors around him.

The achievements of these people were astounding. They were great engineers—aqueducts many miles in length supplied their cities with fresh water, and Montezuma I had built a dam ten miles long, broken by sluice gates for flood control. Three great paved causeways led to Tenochtitlán over its surrounding lakes, and these were so wide that twelve of Cortez's horses could march over them abreast. The empire was covered with a network of hundreds of miles of paved roads, and communication was such that when Cortez landed, the news was carried 250 miles to the capital within a matter of hours.

In science and abstract thought, the achievements of this culture were equally amazing. The Mayas, an earlier Mexican people we shall hear much about, had devised a calendar distinguishing in astronomical terms every separate day for 370,000 years—a feat which would have taken two thousand years of observation. The use of the zero, necessary to all higher mathematics, came to Europe from India about 600 A.D., but the Mayas had devised it for their own mathematical system long before. Moreover, the Aztecs were excellent doctors. They had a full knowledge of human anatomy, and used such medicaments as quinine and digitalis for heart disease. The Spaniards could only admire the hospitals and asylums they kept for wounded veterans.

The Aztec crafts, too, were of a level hardly to be equaled anywhere in the sixteenth century. Some of their textiles were so fine that no modern loom can reproduce them. They were the expert dyers from whom Europe got the use of cochineal.

The Aztecs had a strict code of good breeding. According to Bernal Díaz, "No vainglorious, presumptuous or noisy man has ever been chosen as a dignitary; no impolite, ill-bred man, vulgar in his speaking, impudent in his speech and inclined to say whatever comes into his head has ever sat in their government. And if it should happen that a dignitary makes unsuitable jokes or speaks with levity then he is called a *tecuchechtli,* which means a buffoon." This humility showed itself by moderation in pleasure, by a measured way of speaking—"One must speak calmly, not too fast, nor heatedly, nor loud . . . keep to a moderate pitch neither high nor low; and let your words be mild and serene"; by discretion—"If you hear and see something, particularly something wrong, pretend not to have done so and be quiet"; by willing readiness in obeying—"Do not wait to be called twice: answer at once the first time"; by good taste and restraint in dress—"Do not be too curious in your clothes nor

freakish . . . on the other hand do not wear poor, torn garments"; and by a man's whole bearing—"Walk quietly, neither fast nor slow . . . do not walk with your head down or leaning to one side or looking to right and to left or else it will be said that you are an ill-bred, undisciplined fool."

Justice was sensibly administered in a way unknown in Europe. The emperor appointed the judges, "taking particular care that they were not drunkards, nor apt to be bribed, nor influenced by personal considerations, nor impassioned in their judgements." The laws were strict and strictly maintained, and there were both provincial courts and courts for more weighty matters and of appeal in Mexico City. Scribes carefully noted all cases, with their testimonial and sentences. Sentence was given according to rank: A drunk peasant had his head shaved, but a drunk lord was executed. If the laws were strict, they were in some ways humane. Although drunkenness was a crime punishable by death, the old were allowed and even encouraged to drink to forget their sorrows, and although the Aztecs had slaves, they were carefully protected. Slavery was not inherited, and slaves could only be sold if they were idle or dishonest. Women enjoyed complete equality, and there was a fair system of divorce.

The people were divided into *calpulli,* or clans which owned land communally, but gave it to individual families to use and inherit, as long as it was cultivated. Each clan elected a speaker who represented it in the higher councils of government, and this council, along with the elders of the nation, both men and women, elected the ruler from the royal house. Of course, we recognize this system as a kind of representative democracy. But to the sixteenth-century Spaniards it was totally incomprehensible, so they called Montezuma simply "emperor," a title that would be understood in Europe.

From where did this civilization come? What was its history? Of this we have no record, but that was not the fault of the Aztecs. They possessed a hieroglyphic writing, and they wrote on skins, cotton, and paper made of plant fiber. The profession of historian was taken very seriously, and falsifying history was a capital offense. At Texcoco there was a great library containing, among other things, pre-Aztec records, possibly including an account of a migration from Asia. But the first bishop installed after the conquest burned every book. The earlier Mayas, who had a more advanced script, left a library in Yucatán, and this too was burned. We know, however, that the Aztec culture did not spring full grown. We know that it had a history as long as that of the cultures of Europe and rested on the achievements of many peoples over a period of three thousand years. But what that history was we can tell only by studying the physical remains that are to be found in the more than four thousand ruins and excavations that cover Mexico, and in the development of the superb art of the Mexican peoples.

The first signs of a culture in Mexico date from an era which scholars call the pre-Classical period, from roughly 1800 B.C. to 200 A.D. This was the era that saw, in Europe and the Near East, the Golden Age of Egypt, the rise and fall of Greece, and the growth of the Roman Empire. As we shall see, nearly as much was happening in Central and South America.

During the earliest part of this period, the nomadic hunters of Mexico discovered how to grow maize, and thus they were freed from continuous wanderings in search of food. Soon they learned to cultivate other crops—beans, squashes, melons, nuts, cacao, and various fruits—and to domesticate wild fowl—turkey, geese, ducks, and pheasants. Having settled into villages, they developed other processes to satisfy their needs, such as the making of pottery.

They soon had the leisure to turn their attention toward their spiritual needs and interests. Like the Eskimo and other Indian peoples of the Americas, and in fact like many primitive peoples, the beliefs of the early Mexican tribes were animistic, and they felt that by making little images of women, who to them symbolized fertility, they were creating spirits who would help the crops.

There was a basic similarity in these terra-cotta (baked clay) figurines from every part of Mexico (Plates II-2, II-3, II-4, and II-5). They were all solidly modeled. Great attention was paid to the head and to the thighs, which were exaggerated, but the other parts were treated casually. There was, however, considerable local variation in the style of the detail. In some variations the features were applied as little blobs of clay to the face, the eyes having a slot to represent the pupil; in others the eyes were represented by two triangular impressions while in those from Tlatilco, for example, they are represented by incised almond shapes with a central indentation (Plate II-3). In general, these little figures look as if they could have been made of gingerbread. A slip, or coating of fluid clay, in red or white, was used for color. As time passed sculpture and designs became more ambitious (Plate II-7). Figurines showed people in natural postures; for example, a woman nursing a baby (Plate II-4), or a man seated on a three-legged stool (Plate II-5).

While these changes in art were taking place, around the middle of the pre-Classical period, great changes were taking place in

II-2. Terra-cotta figurines

II-3. Terra-cotta figurine of a woman

II-4. Two terra-cotta female figures (one holding a child)

35

society itself. As the villages grew, some form of organization was necessary. It seemed to be the pattern in Mexico for one man to establish himself as a magician or intermediary with the supernatural; in effect, a shaman. The belief developed that there were especially powerful spirits, or gods, who could only be propitiated by a priesthood. To provide fitting places for the worship of these gods, terraced mounds were built in order to set the temples above the surrounding houses. The earliest of these, at Cuicuilco (Plate II-6), was a circular structure some 440 feet in diameter and about 65 feet high, consisting of four concentric terraces with a system of steps and ramps leading to the top where there must

II-5. Terra-cotta figurine of a seated man

II-6. Terraced temple mound at Cuicuilco

II-7. Pottery figurines in the shape of an acrobat and a vase in the shape of a man

have been a temple of wood and thatch. Here the priests could perform their ceremonies in full view of all onlookers. This was the ancestor of all the many pyramid temples built in Mexico in later centuries, and it bears witness to the great power and organizing ability of the priesthood, even at that early date.

Among the most advanced of the peoples living under a priestly rule in the pre-Classical period from 800 B.C. to 200 A.D. were those who lived at La Venta and Tres Zapotes, two ceremonial centers in the hot, swampy, and forested lowlands of the southeast coast, on the Gulf of Mexico. The name Olmec, "People of the Rubber Country," was applied to them in Aztec times. (As there is no certainty of the continuity of the population from the pre-

Classical period, archeologists prefer to use the term "La Venta culture" to describe them, but the word "Olmec" has been so long applied that one is justified in using it.)

The Olmecs are something of a mystery. There have been many guesses as to their origin, ranging from the tropical lowlands of Tabasco to the highlands of Guerrero. In fact the Olmecs probably came from the region just south of La Venta.

The Olmecs made pottery figures, like the seated child (one of their favorite subjects—the crying child perhaps represented the rain god) in Plate II-8. They were, in fact, the first American people to perfect a technique of firing a hollow clay object. But they were especially known for their work in jade and hard stones. In Plates

II-9, II-10, and II-11 we see finely wrought and highly polished figurines in jade, serpentine, and diopside, all very difficult stones for primitively equipped people to work. We do not know exactly how they cut these stones, but we do know that they had no metal tools. They were probably forced to use string and flat stones aided by abrasives like sand or powdered stone, and later, bone or stone drills, and so we can well appreciate the fine quality of their workmanship. Perhaps because it is the color of water or plant life, jade was valued by the Mexican Indians above all else, certainly above gold and silver.

II-8. Pottery, seated child

II-9. Olmec figures of the pre-Classical period A. Standing figure in diopside B. Standing figure in jade C. Seated figure of a woman

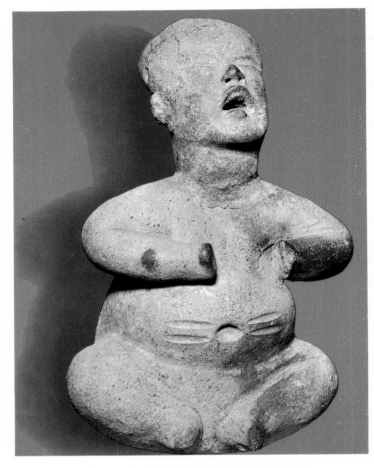

II-10. Seated figure in white jadeite, painted with cinnabar

II-11. Seated figure in jade

When we look at these figurines and the splendid stone funerary masks (which were probably placed on corpses) (Plates II-12 and II-13) the superiority of Olmec sculpture to the little fertility goddesses we have seen is apparent. The Olmec figures are well formed if not perfect. If we look at the central figurine in Plate II-9 we see details of anatomy. The masks show a striking realism, and the features seem to grow naturally from the planes of the face, which are perfectly portrayed.

But if we study these figures carefully we see that there is, all the same, something strange about them. The heads seem elongated and flat, and the lips curl strangely down. This is not the fault of the artist, or some quirk of artistic style. In fact skeletal remains tell us that the Olmecs were short and thickset, with round faces, broad noses, and thick and in all probability drooping lips. Such lips, and they can be quite beautiful, are to be seen in Mexico today. But they are so characteristic of Olmec work that archeologists refer to the "Olmec mouth." Moreover, skeletal remains tell us, too, that the Olmecs deliberately deformed the skulls of newborn infants. This was done by binding the child's head between two boards for several days. The resulting flattened and elongated shape was considered a mark of beauty, and this custom was followed by many later Mexican peoples. Finally, these figures have baby- or child-like proportions and chubby limbs. The reason the Olmecs preferred these child-like shapes in their art is unknown.

We may notice that most of the Olmec figures are without sex. In fact, the Olmecs worshiped, not fertility spirits, but a jaguar god. They probably identified themselves with the jaguar in the way in which the Indians of the Northwest identified with their totemic animals. In Plate II-14 we see a jade figurine of this deity, part human and part jaguar. We see, too, that it has the Olmec mouth, except that here it forms part of a fierce, snarling face. This frightening visage is portrayed again and again on Olmec ceremonial axes. At times (Plate II-15) the face is carved in a fine relief, but more often (Plates II-16 and II-17) it is simplified into an abstract pattern. In portraying spirits, as we have seen

II-12. Stone funerary mask

II-13. Stone funerary mask

II-14. Figure of the jaguar god in jade

II-15. Jade ceremonial axe

II-16. Diopside ceremonial axe

II-17. Ceremonial axe painted with cinnabar

in the work of the Indians of North America, the artist was more interested in arousing emotion than in depicting anything from the visual world. Such axes were probably associated with the thunderbolt. In later mythology it was believed that the gods made lightning by throwing stone axes. There is a cleft in the head of all these axe figures, the meaning of which has never been discovered.

What is most extraordinary is that the Olmecs created large-scale stone sculpture. They covered stone altars (Plate II-18) and monumental upright stones, or *stelae,* with

II-18. Carved stone altar

II-19. Stela with figure of a bearded man

II-20. Stela with figure of a ruler

delicate carving in both high and low relief. On the stela in Plate II-19 there is a bearded man in superbly delicate low relief. In Plate II-20 we see an Olmec ruler in splendid headdress, and the entire stone is covered with a pattern of intricately sculpted barbaric splendor. The Olmecs also decorated stone sarcophagi for their dead (Plate II-21). Here the coffin itself is covered with a flat decorative design, while a figure in deep relief, almost in the round, sits cross-legged in a niche.

These elaborate stone objects lie strewn about the jungle floor, just emerging from the rich vegetation of which they seem a part, and they have a peculiar otherworldly quality, like memories of some mythical jungle kingdom of the imagination. In Plate II-22 a stone monkey looks skyward. Strangest of all are the colossal, almost spherical stone heads (Plate II-23), about eight feet in diameter, placed on the ground without body or even neck, which stood before the Olmec pyramid temples. These carvings portray heavy-jowled people with broad noses and fleshy drooping Olmec lips. On their heads are close-fitting caps resembling a football helmet. Their precise significance is yet another mystery. It is fascinating to note that they seem to be portraits of distinct individuals, perhaps chieftains. These stone heads are all the more amazing in that some of them weigh up to fifteen tons, and the stone came from quarries over sixty miles away. As with the Egyptians, it is a mystery how the peoples of ancient Mexico transported the huge stones with which they built—they did not have wheeled vehicles, nor even pack animals. These weights must have been transported by human strength alone.

But the Olmecs do tell us something about themselves. In Plate II-24 we see the Tuxtla statuette, a jade carving representing

II-21. Stone sarcophagus

II-22. Stone monkey looking skyward

II-23. Colossal head carved in basalt

II-24. The Tuxtla statuette, carved in jade

a duckbilled bird-man. He bears a calendrical inscription corresponding to the date 162 A.D. Later peoples learned both the use of the calendar and a method of inscribing dates from the Olmecs, and this was in fact the beginning of the former's written language. They learned many other things from the Olmecs as well—their deities, the use of pyramid temples, and the technique of creating sculpture on a large scale. They must have learned, too, the tremendous organizational power and division of labor whereby thousands of men could be put to work building the monuments of the splendid temple cities. The Olmecs were the pioneers, and the stage was now set for the great cultures of the Classical period in Mexico.

The Classical period in Mexico lasted during most of the first thousand years of the Christian Era, roughly from 200 to 900 A.D. It was the time when barbarian peoples destroyed the Roman Empire and created a Dark Age in Europe, but in America it was an era of great development. It may be that Mexico in the middle of the first millennium A.D. was the most civilized place on the face of the globe.

Teotihuacán was one of the first and greatest cities of the Classical period. It was built on so splendid a scale that when the Aztecs found its ruins many centuries after its destruction, they called it "Place of the Gods." They felt it could not have been made by man, and so they thought it was the work of giants who lived in some period before the arrival of man on earth. The Aztecs had found some prehistoric mammoth bones, and these they took to be the remains of the builders of Teotihuacán. The early Spaniards, who were no more expert, believed the tale and proudly sent one of the bones to the Emperor Charles V.

Still, when we look at the ruins themselves, we realize why the Aztecs and Spaniards were both confused. The great city spreads over some six square miles, much of the area paved with a plaster floor, on which were erected two huge pyramids, along with many temples and palaces, all connected by great avenues and interspersed with plazas. Much of it is still unexcavated, but the great vistas of clean-lined masonry give one the sense of an almost modern civilization. Moreover, Teotihuacán was probably the first true city in America. Many Olmec settlements and other cities of the Classical period, as we shall see, were built largely as religious centers. But around the great temples of Teotihuacán are the remains of markets and dwellings—those of the priestly nobility and of the artisans who created the city. Farther out, in ancient times, were the adobe houses of the peasants who tilled the fields to support this large and complex society. The city was at the height of its power between 300 and 500 A.D.

The great pile which is called the Pyramid of the Sun (probably in error, as there is nothing about it which suggests worship of the sun) measures almost seven hundred square feet and rises in four terraces to a height of over two hundred feet (Plate II-26). The architects have played several visual tricks on the viewer. The slopes of the pyramid vary in gradient to create an even greater sense of mass, and the stairs going up the slope are wider on

II-25. Map showing the main archeological sites of the Maya Classic and post-Classic civilizations

top than on the bottom, so that their sides appear as two parallel lines, and do not converge toward a vanishing point. This temple was built of adobe bricks from the refuse bed of an earlier era and faced with stone, which in ancient times was covered with smooth plaster. It was built from scratch, and this was unusual: most Mexican pyramids were constructed in Chinese-box fashion, with a newer pyramid covering an older one. An Olmec pyramid has been found under one of a later culture.

Between the Pyramid of the Sun and the smaller Pyramid of the Moon runs a sacred way flanked by the remains of temples and the dwellings of the priests who ruled the city. One of the most striking of these is the temple of Quetzalcoatl, "the Plumed Serpent" (Plate II-27). The temple has gone, but the walls and balustrade of the platform it surmounted are still decorated with massive serpent heads, which were once painted and had fiery eyes of burnished obsidian. On the wall behind the carvings,

II-26. Pyramid of the Sun

II-27. Temple of Quetzalcoatl

the sinewy bodies of snakes appear in low relief and the spaces between the curves are filled with numerous kinds of seashells. Here we see, very clearly, the Teotihuacán architectural style of alternating and contrasting slopes and flat panels, which was to become the characteristic style of all of Mexico. Both this platform and the Pyramid of the Sun were surmounted with simple rectangular temples, supporting crown-like ornaments made of wood and covered with straw and flowers and the brilliant feathers of the quetzal bird, which were the favorite decoration of ancient Mexico.

This was a period when the gods were numerous and all-powerful. Most of the pantheon of gods known to the later Mexican peoples were now worshiped. They were the powerful personifications of the forces of nature: Quetzalcoatl, the plumed serpent, seen here (Plate II-28) with a human face and the body of a snake; Tlaloc, the rain god, portrayed with the mouth of a tiger and circles around his eyes (Plate II-29); Huehueteotl, the god of fire, seen as a wrinkled old man carrying a brazier on his head (Plate II-30). In this figure, which is itself a brazier, we see something typical of the statuary of Teotihuacán—it is severe, formal, and geometric. It reminds us, in fact, of the architecture of the city itself, with its alternating panels, its flat and receding areas. This was true, too, of the splendid murals with which Teotihuacán was painted. These were what are called *frescoes*, pictures painted directly on wet stucco. The colors are shades of red, green, blue, and yellow. Here again the figures have been adapted to flat architectural patterns, but these are the intricate patterns of a tapestry. The elaborately dressed monster in Plate II-31 has a curling shape emerging from his mouth. This means that he is speaking, shouting, or singing. The murals

II-28. Stone sculpture representing the god Quetzalcoatl

II-29. Jade effigy vase of the god Tlaloc

II-30. Brazier carved in the form of the god Huehueteotl

II-31. Fragment of a mural

of Teotihuacán are not only colorful and lively, they are noisy.

As with the Olmecs, the greatest realism is to be seen in the masks of the people of Teotihuacán. Whether made of clay, as in Plate II-32, or stone, as in Plate II-33, these masks were not to be worn by living people, and there are no perforations for the eyes. They were in fact used in funeral ceremonies. Their brows are low and flat to make room for funeral headdresses of brilliant feathers, and they have holes for ear plugs such as were worn by the living. In most of these the features seem triangular and generalized, but in some, like the alabaster mask in Plate II-34, they have the uncanny, living expression of portraits. This mask also bears the mysterious forehead indentation of the Olmec axes. The superb mask in Plate II-35 is inlaid with turquoise mosaic. All such masks would have had inlaid eyes, and here they have been preserved, and the whole has a formal, brilliantly decorative effect achieved by flat panels of color.

The people of Teotihuacán were great innovators. They made charming figurines for offerings and burials, and when the demand for these rose, they developed a technique for mass producing them in molds. Moreover, they discovered for the first time in the western hemisphere the use of the wheel. But, perhaps, because they had no draft animals, they never adapted it to a cart or vehicle of any sort. The wheel was used only on pull toys for children.

The people of Teotihuacán must have been very powerful. Their products are to be found all over Mexico, and their city was unfortified—they feared no enemy. Still, as we shall see, Teotihuacán, like the other capitals of Classical Mexico, came to a violent and mysterious end.

In the rugged mountainous province of

II-32. Painted pottery mask

II-33. Stone funerary mask

48

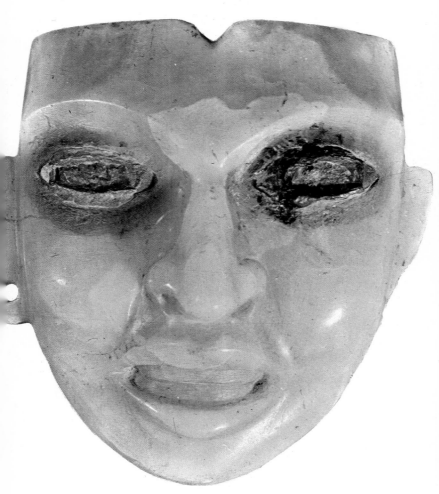

II-34. Alabaster funeral mask

II-35. Funerary mask with turquoise mosaic inlay

Oaxaca there are three broad fertile valleys joined together like the letter T, and thickly spread over them are the dwellings of a people called the Zapotecs. At the junction of the valleys rises Mount Albán, completely detached from the surrounding ranges. The whole of the top of this mountain has been artificially flattened to provide a level platform with an area of about fifteen square miles, the most beautiful ceremonial site in Mexico (Plate II-36), and, some think, the world. On this plateau a vast plaza, all of a mile long and 850 feet wide, stands surrounded by temples set on mounds and terraces, with a temple at its center. It has been said that in a way these ruins make the Acropolis at Athens appear modest and the Roman Forum haphazard.

The culture that created these marvels went well back into the pre-Classical period, when the site of Mount Albán was chosen, and the early inhabitants seem to have been under the influence of the Olmecs. Stone slabs have been found at Mount Albán engraved with figures in active poses, for which reason they are called "The Dancers" (Plate II-37). These figures have the

II-36. View of the ceremonial center of Mount Albán

II-37. One of a series of relief slabs known as "The Dancers"

Olmec mouth and give the general impression of Olmec work. Sometime later, probably at the beginning of the Classical period, the area was invaded by a people from the south, and these are the ancestors of the Zapotecs who built the great monuments.

Mount Albán was not a true city, like Teotihuacán. Rather, it was a religious center, and to its ceremonies there came not only the peoples of the valleys, but possibly pilgrims from as far away as Peru—the religious pilgrimage has a long history in America. It was also a city of the dead, a necropolis, the only one yet discovered in Mexico. Over two hundred tombs have been discovered here, covering the entire side of a hill, and it is in these tombs that the finest art of the Zapotecs has been found.

The Zapotecs created superb funerary urns. At first these were quite simple, but later they were decorated with the squatting figures of dignitaries and gods, with every detail of their immensely elaborate dress and headwear in place (Plates II-38 and II-39). Loaded down with complicated arrangements of jewels and feathers, ear plugs, necklaces, bracelets, collars, and capes, these figures face eternity with all the regal magnificence the imagination of early Mexico could devise. These figures, with their rich projecting decoration and dark shadows, give a heightened sense of the third dimension. In Plate II-40 we see an urn with the figure of a goddess wearing a high square hat made from some textile, and a large pectoral ornament in the form

II-38. Funerary urn with figure of a goddess

II-39. Funerary urn with figure of a seated dignitary

II-40. Funerary urn with figure of a goddess

II-41. Jade pectoral ornament in the form of a bat god

displeased mouth. But perhaps the most striking of all Zapotec works of art is not a funeral urn, but a mask possibly worn as a pectoral ornament, made up of pieces of jade and representing with passionate intensity the bat god (Plate II-41).

Undoubtedly, the greatest of all the cultures of Classical Mexico, the greatest of all cultures in Mexico before Columbus, was that of the Mayas. The Maya culture developed in the area from the peninsula of Yucatán, in southeast Mexico, through the low Petén district of Guatemala to the north of Honduras. This fact alone is amazing. The highlands of Guatemala have rich soil, a temperate climate, and every resource necessary for Maya civilization—obsidian for knives and spears; iron pyrites for mirrors; specular hematite for the much used red paint; jade in the stream beds; the quetzal bird with its greatly prized feathers. Yet the low-lying territory where the Mayas chose to build their great cities is one of the most inhospitable in the world. It is an undulating limestone area, covered in a vast tropical forest crowded with very tall trees—mahogany, cedar, palm, and others. Numerous swamps make communication more hazardous and during the continuous high-rainfall season, from May to December, these become impassable. The soil is thin and poor, and there are few natural resources. Wildlife—jaguars, deer, monkeys, parrots—stays largely hidden from the eye. Until recently the area has lain deserted, infected with the malaria and hookworm that came with the Europeans.

Yet the Mayas cleared the forests and so successfully cultivated their crops of maize that it has been recently calculated that the average Maya farmer worked only 190 days during the year, and in that time produced twice as much corn as his family would

of a *glyph,* a pictograph that may represent her name. There is something infinitely sinister and yet infinitely refined about her beaked nose, her level eyes, and grimacing,

II-42. A. Jade mosaic mask B. Stucco head

need. Thus the Mayas had both the surplus time and the surplus wealth to build a civilization, and build they did—literally dozens of great cities, religious centers built on knolls above the surrounding swamp and joined by hundreds of miles of causeways, bridges, and wide paved roads. These ceremonial cities might be large enough to house 100,000 souls at the time of festivals, and they boasted every wonder from steam baths to pyramids as tall as a modern twenty-two-story office building.

What kind of people were the Mayas? If we look at the jade mosaic mask and stucco head in Plate II-42, we can see that they were physically a very different type from the broad-faced, flat-nosed peoples of the other cultures we have studied. They were a people with long, thin aristocratic faces; they had high cheekbones and large beak-like hooked noses, which they exaggerated by wearing a nosepiece, connecting the bridge with the forehead, so that there appears no indentation at all. In dress they would have seemed a fantasy of richness and color very strange to our eyes. The men

wore a simple loincloth and the woman a sleeveless tubular piece of cloth caught at the waist, but in the case of priests and dignitaries, these garments were richly embellished with plumes, jade beads, and colored shells. Not only were heads deformed, as among other Indians, but crossed eyes were also considered a mark of distinction, and mothers actually hung balls of resin between children's eyes to achieve this. Moreover, ears, lips, and noses were pierced to wear ornaments of jade, wood, shell, bone, and stone. The men wore their hair long, with a bare spot burned on the top of the head, and it was braided and twisted into elaborate headdresses, adorned with flowers, jade, and feathers in the case of the priests, who also wore rows of jade beads around the wrists and ankles, heavy necklaces, and ceremonial capes of elaborate textiles or feathered embroidery. Moreover, the Mayas often painted their bodies and faces, "for the sake of elegance." Boys painted themselves black until marriage, after which they were painted red. Warriors painted themselves black and red, pris-

II-43. Hieroglyphic writing engraved on stone

oners were painted in black and white stripes, and priests were painted blue. In preparation for one of the most important ceremonies of the year, the Mayas painted with blue pigment everything from the utensils of the priests to the spindles with which women wove. We must remember that they were probably extremely neat, and that they bathed daily. The Spanish later swore that they were the cleanest people in the world.

Exotic and decorative though they were, the Mayas had a genius for abstract thought. We have already mentioned that they worked out the use of a zero and a decimal system (or rather a vigesimal system, based on the number 20) long before it was known in the eastern hemisphere. They used this math for their study of the calendar and the passage of time, which was their passion and also a basic part of their religion. Each cycle of time had its own deity, and the calculation of what deity was empowered at what time, and whether well or ill disposed, was an immensely complicated matter. The Maya calendar consisted of a *kin,* or day, a *uinal* (a month of 20 days), a *tun* (a year of 18 uinals, or 360 days), a *katun* (20 such years), and a *baktun* (400 such years). André Emmerich in his *Art Before Columbus* best describes their achievements: "On one monument in the Maya city of Quiriguá, accurate computations sweep back ninety million years; on another, four hundred million years. These are correct computations stating correctly the day and month positions, comparable

for example to calculations in our calendar giving the dates on which Easter would have fallen at equivalent distances in the past. They were made a thousand years before Bishop Ussher in seventeenth-century England placed the creation of the world at 4004 B.C.!"[1]

In Plate II-43 we see Maya script, engraved on stone. These pictographs, or glyphs, are works of art themselves, intricate patterns of design using the sinuous curling line we will see often in Maya art. They were used largely for keeping calendrical records, and it may be that the Mayas never developed a phonetic script because it was necessary for priests speaking different dialects to be able to communicate with one another.

The Mayas well recognized the decorative value of their glyphs, with which they filled every bit of empty space in their reliefs. In Plate II-44 we see a scene from the carved lintel of a temple. In it a kneeling worshiper stands before a serpent god, while, enclosed in geometric areas between the figures and above, we see rows of hieroglyphs. We notice, too, something entirely new. Despite the formal stylization of the entire design, the way the sculptor has presented the figure of the worshiper is unexpectedly realistic. His offerings in his arms and his head turned, he seems, in both proportion and pose, strikingly natural. This is true, too, of the figure in the relief from the Temple of the Sun at Palenque

[1] André Emmerich, *Art Before Columbus,* Simon and Schuster, New York, 1963, pp. 131–132.

II-44. Kneeling worshiper before a serpent god, from a temple at Yaxchilan

II-45. Detail of relief from the Temple of the Sun at Palenque

in Plate II-45. Here not only is the figure tall and correctly proportioned, but his anatomy seems correctly understood, and most difficult of all, the sculptor has succeeded in presenting a foreshortened view of a shoulder, as seen from the side. The Mayas were, in fact, the first of the American peoples to attempt seriously the realistic portrayal of man, and they succeeded with complicated problems like foreshortening and the relaxed portrayal of natural positions of the human body.

What was true of their relief sculpture was also true of their sculpture in the round. The limestone bust of the maize god is realistically formed with arms free of the body and convincingly articulated. The figure itself, with its splendid headdress and heavy ornaments, gives us some idea of what the Mayas themselves must have looked like, fully dressed for a ceremonial occasion (Plate II-46).

The Maya sculptors were particularly known for their *stelae,* rectangular stones sometimes thirty feet high, erected to commemorate some public event. The stele in Plate II-47 shows us that, while interested in realistic portrayal, the Mayas were also masters, as were all the Mexican peoples, at encrusting every inch of a given area with superb, rich decorative detail. Moreover, Maya detail has a rounded, soft, delicate and almost lace-like quality no other peoples possessed. The painted pottery incense-burner in Plate II-48 shows the same delicate detail. It probably represents the sun god, who can be recognized by his filed teeth, the scroll loop over his nose, the pendants hanging from the corner of his mouth, and his vast, staring eyes. He wears a typically complicated headdress comprised of animals, birds, feathers, and beads of jade.

The Mayas were experts in the carving of small jade pieces (Plate II-49), which

II-46. Limestone bust of the maize god

II-47. Stela P

II-48. Painted pottery incense-burner

II-49. Jade plaque portraying a seated dignitary

II-50. Kneeling pottery figurine

they wore in abundance and which they carved with greater refinement than ever seen before. Figurines modeled in pottery were made only before the beginning and at the end of the Classical period. The early figurines were little household gods like those found elsewhere in the pre-Classical period, but the later figurines are more interesting. Most of them come from the area of Campeche, especially the island of Jaina, which must have been a center for the manufacture of such statuettes. These little figures (Plates II-50, II-51, II-52, and II-53) represent members of the ruling class—women, priests, warriors, and civil dignitaries. They are lively and realistic in pose and proportion, and the richness of their apparel and jewelry gives us a picture of a strange but affluent society.

In Plate II-54 we see a cylindrical painted vase of the orange, red, and buff ware common to the Mayas. Here is a chief or priest, sitting on a low platform examining the contents of a basket, while an attendant stands behind him. Again the Maya artist attempts to present the human body in a natural position—in this case the figure is twisting around and leaning over, while squatting on crossed legs—and he has succeeded quite well at an extremely difficult task.

For many years our only knowledge of Maya painting came from such vases and pottery. Then in 1947, an extraordinary discovery was made. In that year the American archeologist Giles G. Healy was taken by the tribe of the Lacandon Indians, descendants of the Mayas, to a ruin they had kept secret since ancient times. In this temple city hidden deep in the jungle, a building was discovered containing three rooms painted with the most splendid pre-Columbian murals ever found. By another stroke of luck, lime-saturated water,

II-51. Pottery figurine of a seated ruler

II-52. Standing pottery figure

II-54. Cylindrical polychrome vase

II-53. Pottery figure of a warrior carrying a shield and wearing a skull trophy

seeping over them, had left them under a coating of stalactite which preserved them perfectly. The newly discovered city was named Bonampak, the Mayan for "painted walls."

Here are depicted scenes of religious ceremonies—festival dances and sacrifice, all performed by elaborately dressed personages. On one wall there is a battle scene (Plate II-55). Maya warriors fiercely and wonderfully arrayed in fantastical plumed headdresses are defeating a foe that has been stripped of clothing. Scenes of warfare are unusual in the art of the Mayas and the early cultures of Mexico. But what is most extraordinary is the way the scene has been painted. Here again we see that the artist has freely portrayed figures in natural, active poses. But he has done something more, he has created a composition with many figures, something never before attempted in Mexican art, to our knowledge, and the total impact of the picture is one of the energetic, furious heat of battle.

In architecture, too, the Mayas were innovators. They developed the corbeled vault to roof stone structures. Such vaults (Plates II-56 and II-57) were created by placing each successive course of stone farther out over both sides of the area to be covered until the two sides finally met. The resulting vault is triangular in shape. The Mayas used this corbeled vault to roof their temples, which stood on stepped pyramids high above the multitude. These temples, several of which are well preserved,

II-55. A battle scene

60

II-56. False arch of the "Governor's Palace"

II-57. Entrance to the Labná Palace

were simple rectangular structures containing one or two small rooms, generally decorated with masks and figures. As we have seen, in other cultures such temples were surmounted with great decorative "combs" of wood and straw. The Mayas translated these combs into stone, which their vaulted temples were able to carry. The Temple of the Sun at Palenque (Plate II-58) has preserved its lace-like ethereal comb. The comb served no practical function, but it made the temple appear all the higher and closer to the gods. The Temple of the Inscriptions in Plate II-59 does not have its comb intact, but it is particularly interesting because, like Egyptian pyramids, it contains the burial chamber of important dignitaries.

The Mayas were also masters of domestic architecture. In Plate II-60 we see the Pal-

II-58. Temple of the Sun

II-59. The Temple of the Inscriptions

II-60. The Palace

ace in Palenque. Such a building might be three stories high, each floor set back behind the lower, with a terrace in front of its windows. The Palace was built around a series of courtyards, and its tower may have been used for the astronomical observations for which the Mayas were so famous.

Towards the end of the Classical period, Maya architecture could be very elaborate indeed. The entire facade of a building might be covered with masks of gods in carved relief (Plate II-61). Those with long projecting "noses" represent the rain god. This building is in the Puuc style. Each of the Maya cities differed from the other in its architecture. Some cities were wealthier and more original, while others seemed to be poorer and more provincial, and to copy their styles from their neighbors. The Puuc style is named for the Puuc foothills in southwest Yucatán, where it originated, and it is considered one of the finest in Maya architecture. The Puuc architects of the late Classic period improved upon all previous Maya practice. Whereas earlier Maya buildings had been constructed of blocks faced with stucco, the Puuc builders invented rubble cores, faced with thin blocks of stone, which were carved before they were built into the facades. These carved stones were fitted together like mosaics in the upper zones of the facade, creating designs of a pristine delicacy. The lower zones were left smooth to give the whole a lighter effect. These structures, as for example, the "Governor's Palace" (Plate II-62) and the building called The Nunnery, at Uxmal, are among the most beautiful in all pre-Columbian Mexico. They have a refinement that only the Mayas could create. The architects of the Puuc style were also the first to replace the earlier heavy pier supports with lighter

II-61. The Kodzpop

II-62. The "Governor's Palace"

63

II-63. View of the quadrangle of "The Nunnery"

II-64. The quadrangle of "The Nunnery"

round and square columns, such as those in the quadrangle of The Nunnery (Plates II-63 and II-64).

The Maya cities we know were not true cities, they were places of worship. Maya art and architecture, like Maya astronomy and mathematics, were devoted to religion. Maya religion was like that of earlier Mexican cultures, but it was more detailed, more elaborately worked out into a complicated scheme of festivals and calculations designed to tell at precisely what moment the gods and cosmic order would be most auspicious for what act, and to propitiate the gods and win their goodwill. To achieve this end the Mayas, so brilliant, tasteful, and even "scientific" though they seem to have been, had a practice which is completely repellent to us: they performed human sacrifice. Yet they cannot simply be written off as barbarous and bloodthirsty, for the Mayas were deeply religious and strict, and the killing formed an integral part of their belief. Utterly dependent for their subsistence, as they imagined they were, they believed the gods only traded their favors for offerings of incense, food, and, above all, human blood. With this they thought the gods would be given strength to perform their tasks.

Even these sacrifices were surrounded with meticulous ceremony and dignity. An auspicious day was selected by the priest, and was preceded by fasting on the part of the officiating priest and principals. On the appointed day, the victim was painted blue, dressed in a peaked headdress, and led to the sacrificial place. The evil spirits were expelled from the worshipers' midst, and the altar smeared with blue paint. The victim was then seized by four *chacs* (elderly lay assistants to the priests). The *nacom* (one of a select group of priests) then advanced, plunged his knife into the ribs above the heart, killing the victim immediately, pulled the heart out, placed it on a plate, and handed it to the officiating priest. The priest then smeared the face of the idol with it. If the sacrifice took place on top of a pyramid, in some ceremonies the chacs threw the corpse down the steps.

Far more agreeable was another ceremony, practiced by the Mayas and all the other Mexican peoples, and called by archeologists "the ball game." The Indian name for the game was *tlachtli,* and it was performed in a court shaped like a capital letter I. One of the best preserved of these courts is in the Zapotec city of Mount Albán (Plate II-65). Set in the wall at either end of this court was a stone or wooden ring, placed vertically, rather than horizontally as in our game of basketball. The players

II-65. Courtyard for the ball game

could strike the hard rubber ball only with their elbows, hips, and legs, and the object was to pass it through the ring. In Plate II-66 we see the Chinkultic disc, a marker for a ball court, and on it is depicted a player kneeling on one knee in order to place the ball on his hip. Needless to say, scoring a goal was rare, in fact so rare that the winners had the right to seize their adversaries' clothing. This all sounds like a great deal of fun, but even the ball game was given ritual and religious meaning. For example, the years before the Spanish conquest were full of evil omens for the Aztecs. To determine whether these predictions were correct, Montezuma played a ritual game of ball, and lost.

II-66. The Chinkultic disc-marker for a ball court

In the little-known coastal area of Vera Cruz, three kinds of stone objects have been found, beautifully carved, and dating from the Classical period. These are known as yokes, hachas, and palmate stones. The yokes were heavy, horseshoe-shaped objects, carved with animal designs (Plate II-67); the hachas were thin, axe-like pieces of stone on which human faces were carved in profile (Plate II-68); and the palmate stones were carvings that stood upright on a narrow base and often carried the effigy of a man (Plate II-69). It was long wondered what these were, but a clue to their use has been found in reliefs on ball courts. In them, players are shown wearing objects like the yokes around their waists, with upright ornaments like the palmates resting on them. Of course these stones could not have been worn during the game, but players might have carried lighter wooden equipment around their waist as protection from the heavy solid-rubber ball. These may be stone replicas made for ceremonial purposes.

The ball game was common to all the Mexican peoples. What, then, was the relationship of these peoples—the Zapotecs, the Mayas, and many others who had so much in common—to each other? It was in fact much like the relationship of the present-day European nations. The peoples of Mexico worshiped the same gods, ate the same food, and dressed and built in much the same manner with strong local variations. They learned a great deal from each other and freely adopted each other's customs. But they spoke different languages, came from different tribal backgrounds, and, like modern Europeans, regarded themselves as separate peoples.

We should mention here that in the little villages of western Mexico far from the great cities where civilizations rose and

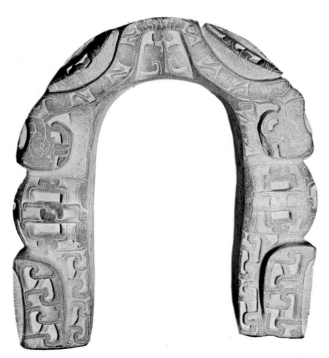

II-67. Carved stone yoke

II-69. Palmate stone in the form of a human head

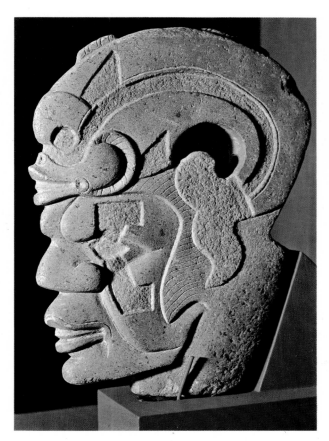

II-68. A basalt axe, or hacha

II-70. Seated couple in pottery

II-72. Seated woman with plate, in clay

II-71. Two seated figures in clay

fell, the life of the peasants changed little, and they too had their art. All during the pre-Classical, Classical, and later periods, while more momentous things were afoot elsewhere, the villages produced charming little figurines—clay statuettes of people going about their daily tasks or just sitting (Plates II-70, II-71, and II-72), perhaps an entire little clay house (or even a village), with all its inhabitants and pets in place (Plate II-73), or a dog scratching its ear (Plate II-74). These figurines served a ceremonial function. But whether they are great art or not, they may make us feel closer to the peoples of ancient Mexico than anything else.

Toward the end of the first millennium A.D. all the great centers of the Classical civilizations were destroyed, many violently. The first to suffer was Teotihuacán. It was sacked and burned about 650 A.D., and its charred stucco and beams are still to be seen. Within the next three centuries Mount Albán was abandoned, and one by one the Maya cities fell. Some were destroyed, others deserted by the middle of the ninth century. It seemed to occur suddenly—pyramids were left without temples and even walls of buildings were left incomplete. Evidently there was no mass migration; the peasants stayed on and made some use of the old centers. Doorways were blocked up once rooms had collapsed, and stelae were dragged round and set up for worship, several upside down, which suggests the worshipers were illiterate. Burials and sacrifices were made among the debris. What had happened? Had the rule of the priests been overthrown by an oppressed peasantry? Or had barbarian invaders destroyed the cities or driven away the inhabitants? Did the murals of Bonampak foretell some final disaster? Possibly both occurred—we do not know.

II-73. Thatched house with inhabitants

II-74. Pottery effigy of a Mexican hairless dog

But by the end of the millennium, throughout Mexico, the rule of the priests had been replaced by the rule of the warriors.

Primitive nomads of great talent and energy swept down into the Valley of Mexico, where Teotihuacán had stood, and established a warrior state. These were the Toltecs. The Toltecs had a legend, which must have much historical basis, that the son of their founder by a princess of ancient priestly stock gave them corn, the calendar, writing, art—in fact, the whole culture of the Classical peoples. This was the Prince Quetzalcoatl, so called because he had studied the religion of Quetzalcoatl, of which he was priest. Quetzalcoatl's rule was a kind of golden age of wisdom and peace, but he incurred the wrath of the priests of the terrible god of war, Tezcatlipoca, the barbaric ancestral deity whom the Toltecs had worshiped in the wilderness. There was a struggle for power, and Quetzalcoatl was banished. He fled to the coast, and there set sail for the Land of the Black and the Red, which must have been Yucatán. But before he left, the fair-skinned, bearded prince swore that he would return by sea from the east to rule again—a fatal threat.

The Toltecs adopted Quetzalcoatl's legacy, the culture of the Classical peoples, but they were very much sons of the god of war. Their religion was centered on human sacrifice, to which the Mayas had resorted only in times of dire necessity. War became a religious necessity for the Toltecs. They needed to subjugate their

II-75. Pyramid of Quetzalcoatl, Tula

neighbors and fight continually so that prisoners of war might be captured to use as victims. Their capital was Tula, situated at a bend in the Tula River in the modern state of Hidalgo, but their campaigns soon took the Toltecs far and wide—as far, in fact, as Nicaragua—and they conquered the old Maya territories of Yucatán. A Toltec tribe called the Itzá subjugated the ancient Maya city of Chichén, which became Chichén Itzá. Here the features of Maya art were incorporated into the new style of the Toltecs, and the sculpture and monuments of Chichén Itzá are the finest Toltec art has to offer.

The artistic style of the Toltecs, like that of the other cultures of Mexico, appeared suddenly, without transition. It was the harsh style of a bloodthirsty warrior people. Tula, like earlier Mexican cities, was built around a plaza some 240 yards square, bounded by pyramids. But Toltec pyramids, like that of Quetzalcoatl at Tula (Plate II-75), differed from earlier ones in that they were lower than Maya pyramids, and were often flanked by colonnaded enclosures, where soldiers congregated to participate in ceremonies. The Temple of the Warriors at Chichén Itzá, with its Court of the Thousand Columns (Plate II-76), is almost an exact replica of this pyramid. The nearby temple which the Spaniards called El Castillo (Plate II-77) is taller, and a triumph of the Mexican religious passion for numbers. It has four flights with 365 steps in all, which bisect the nine levels of the pyramid creating eighteen sections on each side, one for each of the Maya months. One frequent detail of Toltec architecture is the plumed-serpent column, with the serpent's head at its base, and his body curling up behind to support the lintel. We see such columns in Plate II-78.

But despite the fact that the monuments

of Chichén Itzá, built by Maya artisans, are surprisingly light and graceful, a closer look will give us a clearer idea of specifically Toltec art. If we return to the Pyramid at Tula, we will see that on top of it are a series of pillars in the form of warriors, which originally supported the roof beams of the temple (Plates II-79 and II-80). Warriors were a favorite subject of Toltec sculptors, and warrior figures are often used as supports for heavy architectural parts. These figures are rigid, stiff, geometrical, and heavy—a far cry from the fluid patterns and delicate detail of Maya art. They wear butterfly breastplates that have been stylized to a foursquare pattern, and round shields are strapped to their waists in back. Even the feathers of their headdresses are stiff,

II-76. Temple of the Warriors

II-76. Court of the Thousand Columns

II-77. Pyramid called El Castillo

II-78. Temple of the Warriors

II-78. Temple of the Warriors showing plumed-serpent columns

II-79. Pillars in the form of warriors from the Temple of Quetzalcoatl

II-80. Rear view of the pillars of the Temple of Quetzalcoatl

II-81. Stone warrior

II-82. Stone figure from the Temple of the Warriors

II-83. Chac Mool figure

and they stare out at us with the vacant look of automatons. And yet there is a certain strength and simplicity about these figures that Maya works perhaps lack.

Squareness was typical of Toltec art. Heavy figures like those in Plates II-81 and II-82 supported altars and tables. A squared-off recumbent figure of Chac-Mool, attendant of Tlaloc, the rain god, supporting a receptacle on his stomach, was a favorite form (Plate II-83). These figures, lolling on their backs, are thought to have the easy shape of drifting clouds. The famous red-cinnabar painted jaguar throne from Chichén Itzá is a magnificent and powerful piece of rectangular sculpture (Plate II-84). Spotted with jade discs, its teeth are made of white flint. This was a fit throne for the sun.

In reliefs, curved scrolls are combined with linear geometric and step patterns, and we feel that the Toltecs adapted other peoples' designs and combined them without discrimination (Plate II-85). Such reliefs, some of which are very fine (Plate II-86), often present a flat, unmolded surface, with sharply cut edges.

Moreover, the Toltecs had a taste for grisly subject matter. Snakes and human skulls (Plate II-87) become a common motif. The Toltecs had warrior orders of the Jaguar and the Eagle, rather like medieval European knightly orders. The knights wore helmets in the form of jaguars (representing the earth) and eagles (representing the sun), and eagles and jaguars are now seen in reliefs, devouring human hearts (Plate II-88).

The Toltecs devised a particularly horrible form of monument, which often stood next to their temples. This was the *tzompantli*, a stone platform supporting a wooden rack on which the skulls of sacrificial victims were placed. In Plate II-89

II-84. Jaguar throne

II-85. Relief detail from the facade of the Temple of Quetzalcoatl

II-86. Relief from wall of the great ball court

II-87. Detail of relief from the ball court showing skulls

II-88. Stela with relief representing a jaguar holding a human heart

we see the Tzompantli at Chichén Itzá, engraved with skulls on all four sides.

Chichén Itzá was the site of the great Cenote (Plate II-90), the sacred well to which people came from all over Central America to make sacrifices. Cenotes are large apertures where the limestone crust of the earth has caved in to expose a pool below, and they are the main source of water in this area. The great Cenote was sacred to the rain god, and worshipers came to throw sacrificial objects of great value into it. Human victims were thrown in as well, a fall of sixty-five feet, with instructions to carry prayers for rain to the gods. Should anybody survive he was pulled out in the belief that the rain god

II-89. The Tzompantli

II-90. The Cenote of Sacrifice

had sent him back with a message. One man, Hunac Ceel, is said to have dived in and survived. He was held in great honor for this feat and became the ruler of Chichén Itzá.

In 1900 Edward H. Thompson, the American consul, set about dredging the well. He found, apart from human remains, a treasure of objects, some in bronze and gold, from Panama and Costa Rica. Such little cast figurines (Plate II-91) are of great importance. They are the first evidence of metalwork in Mexico and of bronze and gold, which were common and had been worked for centuries farther south in Central and South America. Since Thompson's day, divers and dredgers have found a great deal more treasure.

Toltec rule did not last for long. Tula was abandoned in 1168, and finally de-stroyed in 1224. Again we might ask why. The reasons are not hard to find. The Toltecs had abandoned agriculture and lived on the tribute of conquered states from which they took their sacrificial victims. It is easy to see how, threatened themselves by barbarian tribes from the north, they had few allies on which they could depend. Chichén Itzá survived longer, but its power in Yucatán eventually fell to a city called Mayapán. This was a new kind of city: A wall was built around the ceremonial quarter and the citizens, rather than living in the surrounding countryside, huddled together in a warren-like cluster of dwellings crowded within the walled defenses. Mexico was heavy with fear and the danger of attack.

After the fall of the Toltec empire, central Mexico was invaded by Chichímec nomads from the north, and a number of small states developed, in which the barbarism of the newcomers was merged with the religion and skills of the older civilizations.

The Aztecs, or Mexica, as they called themselves, were the last of the immigrant tribes to reach the Valley of Mexico. A ragged pack of nomads, they wandered about seeking a place to settle, offering their services as mercenaries, stealing women from their neighbors, and generally arousing the enmity of everyone by their behavior. At one point they were even enslaved.

They eventually won their freedom, but it was not until 1325 (according to one source) that they found a permanent abode. The first of many shrewd decisions, they chose a swampy but easily defensible island on the shores of Lake Texcoco for the site of their city, Tenochtitlán. They had accepted the overlordship of the powerful city of Azcapotzalco, but in 1428, they successfully rebelled in company with other tribes, and out of this revolt there grew the triple alliance of the Aztecs with the people of Texcoco and Tlacopán, in which the Aztecs became the dominant power. The alliance established a leadership over the whole of Mexico from the Gulf Coast to the Pacific. The Aztecs

II-91. Gold figures dredged up from the Cenote of Sacrifice

could only have accomplished this by the most clever diplomacy, a well-disciplined policy, and great skill in war as well as cold-blooded cruelty. They were, in fact, the first people in North America to use war to deliberately build an empire.

When they first established their city, the Aztecs made one other shrewd decision. They took as their royal family the last descendants of the Toltec dynasty, giving them legitimate claim to the fallen Toltec empire. They also adopted many Toltec regal customs, including the ceremony of investiture. And so, in Toltec tradition, when he ascended the throne, every Aztec ruler was told "Remember that this is not your throne but only lent to you, and that one day it will be returned to Quetzalcoatl, to whom it truly belongs."

As we have seen, the Aztecs developed political and legal institutions of great wisdom, superior to anything to be found in Europe at that time. And yet there was another side to their character that was altogether appalling. Like the Toltecs, all their efforts were turned towards war. Their priests were also warriors, and the highest award a man could hope to attain was to be made an Eagle knight or a Jaguar knight. Their powerful corporations of merchants, a sort of middle class, went on trading expeditions throughout Central America, but they too were military spies, and their misadventures were often used as excuses for military expeditions. Finally, apart from sheer power, a major motive of Aztec warfare was the need to provide human hearts for the nourishment of the gods. The Aztecs believed that without the sacrifice of men the power of the gods waned until they could not renew the annual cycle of fertility of the earth. Human sacrifice was the central rite of Aztec life. No god could be questioned on any subject,

no festival of the calendar celebrated, without countless immolations—more and more each year. By the time the Spanish arrived the practice had reached such proportions that there were twenty thousand victims annually. Death by sacrifice came to be an expected and even desirable end, for which poetry and religion both prepared the victim.

The Aztecs were like the Romans in their sense of justice and moderation in most matters, but like the Romans, their personality was split and they had a taste for public slaughter. Like the Romans, too, they took their culture and their art from earlier peoples. The Aztecs possessed the best in sculpture, pottery, lapidary work, textiles, in fact, all the material arts that cater to the demands of a wealthy populace. They were the heirs to the achievements of many civilizations and they could draw on the craftsmanship of all the conquered peoples of their empire.

Tenochtitlán, the city of Mexico, as Cortez found it, was the culmination of three thousand years of monumental building. Of it, not one stone remains. But from early accounts and from traces of foundations found when undertaking new work in the modern city, archeologists have been able to reconstruct a picture of what it must have been like. It differed from all previous urban layouts in the Valley of Mexico. The sacred precinct was walled round, and it was overshadowed by a much larger residential city and suburbs. Thus "the city of the gods" shrank to a central area dedicated to temples, set among the dwellings of men. Its most important building was the great twin temple of Tlaloc and Huitzilopochtli, with its two shrines set on one enormous stepped pyramid, and approached by twin stairways. This must have been very similar in form to

II-92. The pyramid at Tenayuca

tuc temple at Tenayuca (Plate II-92). In front of it was a great plaza upon which was set the stone of sacrifice, where victims were tethered to fight an unequal combat against warriors armed with obsidian weapons. Nearby was the temple of Quetzalcoatl, circular in shape so that it would offer less resistance to the wind, as Quetzalcoatl was also a wind god. Its entrance portal was through the opened jaws of a serpent. The Aztecs also built ball courts like those at Chichén Itzá, and there was a tzompantli, or skull rack.

To increase the size of their original island the Aztecs adopted an ingenious system of reclaiming land. They made great baskets which they floated into place, and filled with earth. On these they grew crops and gradually the accumulation of silt below and vegetable mold on top consolidated them. These were the famous *chinampas,* or floating gardens, which the Spaniards described. Tenochtitlán was therefore a sort of Venice intersected by canals. The Aztecs were always systematic, and an early map shows the city to have been laid out on a rectangular plan with streets and canals crossing at right angles. The ordinary houses, usually painted red, were built round a patio with a plaster floor.

The most important remains that we have of Aztec art are stone sculptures. It is little wonder that these absolutely terrified the Spanish. They were often colossal in scale, like the great effigy of Coatlicue, mother of the gods, which stands some eight feet tall. Coatlicue was the goddess of the earth, and of the underworld. Her head is formed of two snakes, her necklace of human hearts and hands, her skirt is made of writhing serpents, and she has the paws of a jaguar (Plate II-93). In other statues she is shown as a rather playful and

II-93. Stone figure of Coatlicue

II-94. Figure of Coatlicue

kittenish creature, with a skull for a head (Plate II-94). Quetzalcoatl, a more benevolent deity, is sometimes represented as a human head in the jaws of a coiled rattlesnake, whose body is covered with graceful, drooping feathers (Plate II-95). In his manifestation as Ehecatl, the wind god, he is represented as a naked figure, clad only in a loincloth, but with an enormous mouth like the bill of a duck (Plate II-96), a survival of the duckbilled god of ancient days. If these figures seem a composite of monstrosities, we still must admire their fine workmanship, and admit that they are forceful, even brutal, in their impact.

The grimmest of all these stone gods,

II-95. Stone figure of Quetzalcoatl

II-96. Statue of Ehecatl

perhaps, is Xipe Totec, "Our Lord the Flayed One," the personification of the force for rebirth in nature. In the spring months at planting time, a youth chosen to represent Xipe was sacrificed and flayed. His skin was then worn as a costume by a priest, as a symbolic enactment of the live seed within the dry husk. In Plate II-97 we see a figure of the seated god Xipe Totec as a priest. He is shown wearing a victim's skin, identified by the slit over the heart, and we see the live priest peering sinisterly out through the eyes of the dead.

But, as with everything Aztec, there is also another side to Aztec art. It is perfectly exemplified in Plate II-98. On the

II-97. Seated figure of the god Xipe Totec

II-98. A. Mask of Xipe Totec   B. Head of an Eagle knight

A   B

left is a mask of Xipe Totec, wearing a human skin—bloated and soulless, in no way a human figure. But on the right is a portrait of a helmeted Eagle knight—a softly modeled, sensitive portrait of a man. Nor were all the Aztec gods without charm. Xochipilli was the god of flowers, music, song, and dance. In Plate II-99 we see him seated cross-legged on a throne decorated with flowers and a wavy line to indicate the rhythm of music and verse. He is in a pose of contemplation and abstraction. The figure of Xochipilli in Plate II-100 has cocked his head to one side, as if lost in a dream of appreciation of some moving piece of music.

These mysterious people loved poetry, and their language was beautiful and expressive. Certain Aztecs were taught the Latin script by early Spaniards, and so some of their prose, their laws, their moral precepts, and their poems were written down after the conquest and survive. Dancers, poets, and musicians were kept by the nobles and performed a major part in the rituals of religion. Their lyric poetry was obsessed not only with death, but with flowers; here is a poem from the city of Chalco:

II-99. Statue of Xochipilli

Vainly you seize your flowered *teponaztli,*
You throw handfuls of flowers; but in vain.
They wither.
We too, we are here singing our new song,
And there are new flowers, too, in our hands.
    May our friends delight in the flowers.
    May the sadness fade out of our hearts.
    Let no one be overwhelmed by sadness.
    Let no one's thoughts wander about over the earth.
    Here are our precious flowers and songs.

May our friends delight in them.
May the sadness fade out of our hearts.
O friends, this earth is only lent to us.
We shall have to leave our fine poems,
We shall have to leave our beautiful flowers.
That is why I am sad as I sing for the sun,
We shall have to leave our fine poems.
We shall have to leave our beautiful flowers.

II-100. Statue of Xochipilli

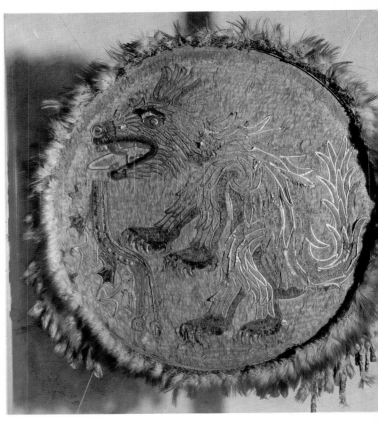

II-101. Feather mosaic shield

Montezuma's tribute list, which is still perserved in the National Museum in Mexico, gives us some idea of the vast and colorful wealth of the Aztecs. The list consists of name-glyphs of groups of towns, and pictures of the commodities with numerals indicating the quantities that were due. It is an incredible document: 140,000 bushels of corn, 36,000 bundles of tobacco, 48,000 sheets of paper, 187,560 *loads* of blankets (Aztec embroidery was superb, but all examples have been lost). A surprising item was 32,880 bundles of quetzal and other gaily colored feathers from the tropical areas of southern Mexico. These were used to make gorgeous feather headdresses, the feather war-standards, and marvelous feather mosaic ceremonial shields. In Plate II-101 we see such a shield, with the figure

of a blue plumed coyote, another whimsical Aztec beast, outlined in gold. This shield was actually a gift of Montezuma to Cortez; only six such examples of Aztec feather mosaic remain in the world.

The list also includes Spondylus shells and little baskets of turquoise, for inlay work. There were completed objects of superb turquoise inlay also from the Mixtecs, a powerful tribe which had driven the Zapotecs out of Monte Albán in Oaxaca, and were never entirely conquered by the Aztecs. These were made by setting tiny fragments of turquoise, some no more than a sixteenth of an inch across, in gum over a core of wood (Plates II-102 and II-103). They are perhaps the most strangely exotic and colorful of all the Aztec treasures. It is thought that the turquoise snake in Plate

II-102. Mask of Tlaloc in turquoise mosaic

II-103. Effigy of Tlaloc in turquoise mosaic

II-104 and the mask in Plate II-105 were sent by Montezuma to Cortez, who sent them on to the Emperor Charles V. The Mixtecs, too, sent objects of the fine goldwork for which they were famous, made by the *cire perdue* method. In *cire perdue* (French for lost wax) casting, a wax model is sculpted over a central core or supporting foundation of clay; it is then packed with a thick coating of clay and heated. Under sufficient heat the outer shell of clay hardens, while the middle layer of wax melts and runs out through a spout penetrating the outer shell. Molten metal is then poured into the space left by the melted and drained wax between the clay core and the outer covering. After cooling, the clay and spout are then carefully chipped away and the sculpture is finished (Plate II-106).

Pendants like these, gold ear plugs, gold dust, and jade beads were all part of the trappings of barbaric splendor which found their way to Tenochtitlán, together with such items as live eagles and rubber balls.

It was to this vast and rich empire that the news came in April 1519, at a dire period in the Aztec calendar, that a fair-skinned bearded stranger, arrived by ship from the east, had come to seize the empire. There was no doubt in the mind of Montezuma—Quetzalcoatl had returned.

And so Cortez, with 633 men, sixteen horses, thirty-two crossbows, and thirteen cannon-like muskets, conquered a wealthy civilization of millions, a civilization of warriors. How did he succeed? He succeeded because the Aztec leader was paralyzed by superstition, or perhaps by faith.

II-104. **Double-headed serpent in turquoise mosaic**

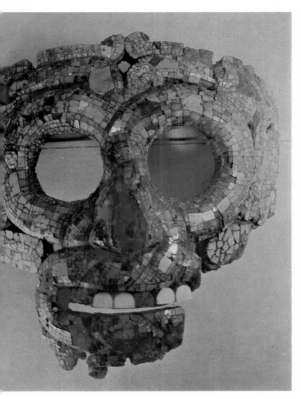

II-105. Mask in turquoise mosaic

II-106. Gold pendants

He succeeded, too, because the Aztecs had never seen a horse, or firearms, and both terrified them. (They believed that the cannon were inhabited by evil spirits, and that they fired themselves at will.) But most important he succeeded because many of the peoples of the empire, so long oppressed, joined the Spaniards and rose against the Aztecs and their relentless thirst for blood. Quetzalcoatl, the Prince of Peace, had not returned, but by some strange twist of fate the myth of his return avenged his banishment.

The fall of Tenochtitlán was the fall of all the civilizations of ancient Mexico. The city itself, the city of palaces and floating gardens, cool courtyards, and mighty pyramids, was dismembered stone by stone and thrown into the canals. In his old age Bernal Díaz wrote:

"I say again that I stood looking at it, and thought that no land like it would ever be discovered in the whole world. But today all that I saw is overthrown and destroyed; nothing is left standing."

The Art of the Ancient Cultures of Peru

THE STORY OF the great civilizations of Mexico and their conquest is extraordinary, but the fact that this story should have been repeated in South America seems beyond belief, and yet it was so. When in May of 1532 Francisco Pizarro arrived at Tumbes on the coast of Peru with an army of 180 men and 27 horses, he was to discover an empire mightier, and in some ways even more amazing, than that of the Aztecs in Mexico—the empire of the Incas.

Cuzco, the capital of the Inca Empire, was a city to match or surpass any in Mexico. Brilliantly painted buildings of red and yellow, perhaps a hundred thousand of them, housed citizens from every corner of the empire, each wearing the distinctive, colorful dress and decoration of his tribe. Pure water flowed through stone conduits in the streets, and the town was laid out along a gridiron plan around two central plazas, the largest of which was called the Plaza of Joy. The great temples and palaces of the city were built of huge interlocking boulders of finely fitted stone, and these were not decorated with sculptural or painted patterns as they were in Mexico, but were sometimes plated with solid gold. Most amazing, for sheer splendor, was the Golden Enclosure, the Curi-cancha, with its adjoining Temple of the Sun. Here stood six sanctuaries—to the sun, moon, stars, lightning, and the rainbow, with a house for the priests of the sun— surrounding the Field of the Sun, a creation so incredible that, had it not been seen by several eyewitnesses from Europe, it would certainly be thought to be a myth. In the

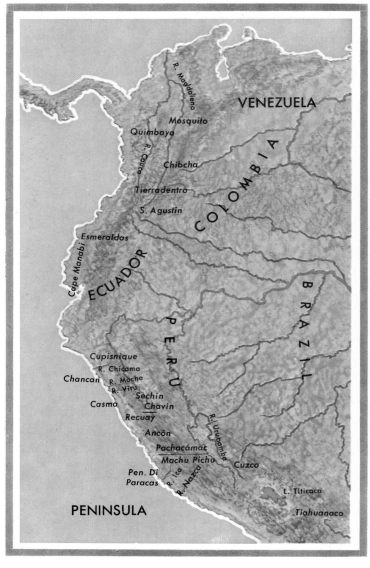

III-1. Map of the cultural areas of the Andes

Field of the Sun, the world of the Inca was translated into solid gold. From golden clods of earth grew whole cornfields of golden maize, while life-sized shepherds of gold were set with slings and crooks to watch over a herd of twenty llamas, all of solid gold. Pizarro's men braved the heights of the Andes and enemies numbering in the millions to conquer Peru, and like the followers of Cortez in Mexico, they were rewarded with sights no European had expected to see short of paradise.

Cuzco was but one of many cities of the empire of Peru, which stretched along the

Pacific from what is now Ecuador to what is now Chile, in an area that would seem inhospitable to civilization. On the coast, because of currents and mountain formations, there runs a parched desert. To the east, dense jungles descend into the valleys of the Amazon, and between the shore and the jungle there rises the backbone of the Andes mountains, among the highest in the world. And yet by means of the most impressive feats of engineering, the Incas had turned this forbidding terrain into a rich and flourishing empire.

The many towns and cities of the empire were united by a superb system of wide and often paved roads. Two main highways ran north and south, along the coast and highlands respectively, and these were joined by smaller roads that extended to every village in the empire. Like Roman roads, these were as straight as possible, and the coastal highway was twenty-four feet wide. The roads were carried over marshes on causeways and over streams on bridges. These extraordinary structures were sometimes made of pontoons, or, for shorter spans, stone slabs supported by masonry piers. Wide expanses were spanned by suspension bridges of rope cables. Hills might be tunneled through, and in irrigated valleys the roads were lined with stone walls and planted with shade trees. Well-stocked rest houses greeted official travelers at regular intervals. Along these roads the Lord-Inca might travel to survey his empire, sitting in a golden litter set with precious stones, and couriers running in relays could cover 250 miles a day. They carried fresh fish for the emperor in Cuzco from the coast.

The precipitous land of the Andes could not be cultivated unless it was carefully terraced and irrigated (rains were unreliable), and the Incas were experts at both. Irrigation ditches were often many miles in length, following the contours of the hills, and where necessary they were lined with stone. There were also great reservoirs, as well as stone-lined underground sewers. Over low parts irrigation ditches were carried on causeways; one in the Moche Valley was over fifty feet high. Small sluices controlled and closed by stone slabs led from the main channel to the fields. In some places water was led to the top of a series of hillside terraces and allowed to flow over them; the terraces, which in certain areas covered the hillsides, were supported by long parallel retaining walls, and many of these Inca terraces still stand today, reshaping the landscape into a strange series of flat plains. They provide more arable land than would otherwise be possible, and prevent erosion. When the Incas conquered new territory, models were made of terraces, buildings, arable land, and even towns to guide the Inca engineers.

With these techniques, and with the aid of fertilizers, the Incas produced a wonderful abundance of food. No less than half the foods eaten in the world today were cultivated by the Andean Indian, many especially developed by "professionals" in the hire of the Lord-Inca. These included forty varieties of potato, twenty varieties of corn, and all known beans except the broad bean and soybean, as well as manioc (from which we get farina), peanuts, cashews, pineapples, chocolate, avocados, tomatoes, peppers, strawberries, and many others. Guinea pigs were kept for meat, and the llama worked as pack animal and provided a rough wool for sacks and blankets, while its cousin the alpaca provided finer wool for clothing. And so the Incas, lacking, as did the Aztecs, both the horse and the wheel, built a splendid material civilization without them. Inca cities, with their palaces, storehouses, fortresses, and temples of the sun, were to be found in an area that stretched over more than three thousand miles of South America. This was Tahuantinsuyu, the Four Quarters of the Earth, as the Incas called their empire.

But what was probably most exceptional about the Incas was their sense of social organization. The people we call "the Incas" were not a nation, or even a ruling caste, but actually a ruling family. The Lord-Inca himself, the head of the family, called simply *the* Inca, was thought to be a divinity on earth, the actual son of the sun. He ate from vessels of silver and gold, wore only tunics of the finest wild vicuna wool, which were destroyed when they had once been on his back, and his very word was law—in theory all belonged to him. His first wife was his own sister, so that her children were of the pure line of the sun, but he had hundreds of concubines and hence an enormous family, from which were drawn the chief administrators of the land, the Incas by blood. These ruled with the aid of silversmiths, goldsmiths, weavers, accountants, priests, architects, and engineers—those very "professionals" who were sent out to methodically plan the cities, roads, and irrigation works of the empire.

The people over whom the Incas ruled are called the Quechuas as Quechua was their tongue. These "people of the warm valley" were conquered early by the Incas, who adopted their language and brought it to the many other peoples of the Andes whom they later incorporated into their empire. It is still spoken today throughout the entire area.

What was most remarkable, however, was that the Inca, the type of absolute ruler who might well have developed into a despot, seems to have obeyed the injunction of the sun god to rule with "reason and justice, with benevolence, clemency, and kindness." The land of the empire was controlled by the local village, or *ayllu,* very like the Mexican calpulli. The land of each ayllu was divided into three parts, one part belonging to the Inca, one part to the priests, and one part to the farmers. At the beginning of the year each man was given all the land he needed to support his family, and all the land of the ayllu was worked communally. Thus the farmer paid his tax by working the Inca's land. He also paid it by working on government projects such as roads, water systems, and mines. All men were married at the age of twenty, and those who had not chosen a bride were supplied with one. Thus the common man's life was completely controlled from beginning to end.

But every man was given, too, complete security. The Inca supplied each family with enough alpaca wool to keep it warm, and when crops failed, those farmers who were lacking were fed from the Inca's granaries. Farmers in one area were given the produce of another, so that their diet would be varied. Above all, there was to be no hardship. Work in the mines was considered unpleasant, so mine workers were constantly rotated, and provision was made so that they could be accompanied to the mining area by their wives. Moreover, as in Mexico, the law was stricter for a nobleman than for a commoner. If a man was caught stealing for want, it was the administrator, who was to see to it that all his needs were fulfilled, who was punished. Diversion, too, was provided. "So that labor might not be so continuous as to be oppressive," the Inca ordained that there should be three holidays a month, when the people should entertain themselves with games and drinking, and three fairs a month at which they could hear the decrees of the Inca and his councils, and exchange goods (there was no coinage in the ancient Americas). Moreover, there were great monthly public festivals, with names such as the Garment of Flowers, and the Dance of Young Maize, at which the common farmer was stupefied with a display of rich gold costumes, and singing and dancing of all kinds. Such, then, was the rule of the Incas.

What was the history of the Inca Empire? At this point we come to one of the great distinctions between the empire of the Incas and those of the peoples of Mexico. Whereas the Mexicans had possessed the art of writing for the millennia, and kept careful and respected records of their history, the Incas and the Andean Indians seem to have had no form of writing to speak of (although it has recently been proposed that certain repeated patterns on textiles, thought to be decorative, represent a kind of Inca script). The Incas kept all records, including those of their history, by means of an intricate knotted-string technique, known as *quipu*, and what the knots on these strings indicated about Inca history could be interpreted by professional "rememberers." What did these rememberers in fact remember?

They remembered that many ages ago a fair-skinned man came who had "great power over nature." He raised mountains and brought water forth from the rocks, and was called Viracocha, the Creator and the Beginning of All Things and the Father of the Sun. He left the land of Peru, striding forth on the sea as if it were dry land, but he promised to return. It was the sun god, they said, who created the first Inca, Manco Capac, and his sister on the Isle of the Sun in Lake Titicaca. These two then wandered north to found a city at a place where, according to the instructions of the sun god, the soil was so soft and

deep that a golden staff thrown into the ground would totally disappear. This was Cuzco.

Thus far this account seems a fair mixture of myth and fact. The Incas did come from the area of Lake Titicaca to found Cuzco at about 1100 A.D., and make it the center of their ever-expanding empire. But the rememberers go on to say that the sun god also instructed the Inca and his family to bring civilization to the savages among whom they lived. This was not a fact of history lightly cloaked in mythology—it was a simple historical lie. Archeology tells us that Inca civilization, like that of the Aztecs in Mexico, rested on the shoulders of many cultures, going back more than two thousand years. The Incas had deliberately chosen to obliterate the memory of these cultures from history. Their rememberers had no recollection of them, and the Incas had virtually nothing to tell the Spaniards of the earlier Peruvian peoples. Thus we can know these cultures only through what we can gather from archeological remains, and often we cannot even tell what these peoples called themselves. But we do know that they developed, slowly and with great care, the splendid tradition of art that Pizarro and his men found throughout the Inca Empire.

The earliest cultures of Peru developed not in the high Andes, but in the deathly deserts of the coast, cut by rich river valleys where men could settle. These valleys were ideal for man: They were rich with silt brought down from the Andes, and the fish-eating seabirds of the coast left deep deposits of guano, the richest fertilizer in the world. Moreover, although it never rains on this coast, the temperature is mild and where the soil is watered by rivers, there might be several crops a year. It was here that during the second millennium B.C., at roughly the time of the first settled agricultural life in Mexico, early traces of human settlement were later found in the great shell mounds of Huaca Prieta, where people who were partly farmers, partly fishermen, threw their refuse. The art of making pottery had already developed, and these people wore simply patterned warp cloths with snake-like designs of brown and white cotton; sometimes they were dyed blue and rubbed with a red pigment. Nobody knows where these first Peruvian people came from, but the designs on these textiles show so high a level of culture, appearing suddenly, that it is thought they must have come from elsewhere. Precisely where, however, is a mystery archeologists have yet to solve.

This early age of the farmers was followed, during the first millennium B.C., by a period which archeologists call the Early Horizon. The word "horizon" is used to mean a period dominated by the broad spread of a single style of art, and the art of this era, and its religion, came from the single center of Chavín de Huántar, in the northern highlands. (The settlers in the river valleys leading from the Andes to the Pacific were in touch not so much with the other river valleys of the coast, from which they were separated by impassable desert, as with the peoples upriver, in the highlands near the coast.) At this religious center there have been found steeply walled platforms, honeycombed with stone-lined passages around a sunken central court. The walls of these structures were made of roughly dressed stone and decorated with stone heads of men, and of the terrifying god with cat-like characteristics which the people of the Chavín cult worshiped, along with other somewhat feline monsters. Standing about are stone carvings, many of human figures with the canine teeth of

jaguars and with snake-like appendages. Like many of the religious centers of Mexico, this was not a town, but a holy place to which pilgrims came from a wide area and possibly stayed for a while to assist in works of piety, like building walls or even carving figures.

Thus the art style of Chavín, complicated and forceful, spread to many parts of Peru. At Cupisnique, for example, in the Chicama Valley on the north coast, we find pottery in the style of the stone carvings of Chavín. In Plate III-2 we see such a vessel, with a heavily incised geometric design. This pot has a thick spout shaped like a stirrup, which branches out and offers two entrances to the jar. The purpose of such a spout was to facilitate the flow of water through one hole by allowing air to enter

III-2. Stirrup-spouted vase of the Early Chavín culture

94

III-3. Paracas textile fragment showing deity
with serpent staves

through the other. This shape remained typical of Peruvian pottery until the arrival of the Spanish, and we shall see it again and again.

At this time a strange culture developed on the Paracas Peninsula, one of the archeological mysteries of all time. Here, in deep caverns in the desert sands, close to the sea, were found four hundred mummies, well preserved in the arid atmosphere, and superbly dressed in turbans, shawls, and robes. We know nothing of the civilization that produced these mummies—neither how they lived nor who ruled them nor even what they called themselves. No other culture has left any record of them. We know only what they wore: splendid jewelry and clothing of the most elaborately and finely woven cloth ever loomed by man.

These textiles were worked in an almost infinite variety of colors to depict human forms, heads, monstrous creatures, snakes, and birds, all converted into immensely complicated flat patterns. No subject was beyond the ingenious skill of the Paracas weaver. In Plate III-3 we see a deity holding two staves in the form of serpents. Such figures would be repeated again and again in even rows, but with differing colors, as we see the figures in Plate III-4. This woven band with a scalloped edge was a kind of ribbon, probably worn as a headband to keep hair or a cloth in place. The figures are that of the partially human god surrounded by jagged serpents. The fragment in Plate III-5 shows us that such designs were sometimes pieced together on plain cloth to form a checkered pattern.

In Plate III-6 we see what must have been part of a poncho or similar garment in brown fabric embroidered with trophy heads, and trimmed with a purple fringed border. More elaborate still is the involved design we see in Plate III-7, which obviously has a religious purpose. It is made up of heads of gods, with snakes and feline animals.

But we must remember that the people of the Paracas culture lived by the sea, and perhaps most decorative of all is the textile fragment we see in Plate III-8, depicting the killer whale in a sea of brilliant red (representing water suffused with blood?).

Meanwhile, sometime shortly before the first millennium A.D., the power of the cult of Chavín melted away, although its feline gods remained as the religious motif of later peoples. A new era, called the Early Intermediate period—during which great advances took place in pottery and the art of weaving—now began. Red pottery, painted in white, was now common, and many shapes, including those of human

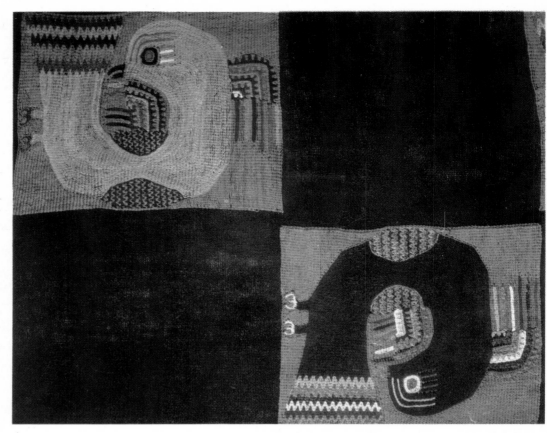

III-5. Paracas fragment of a poncho showing figures of birds in a checkered pattern

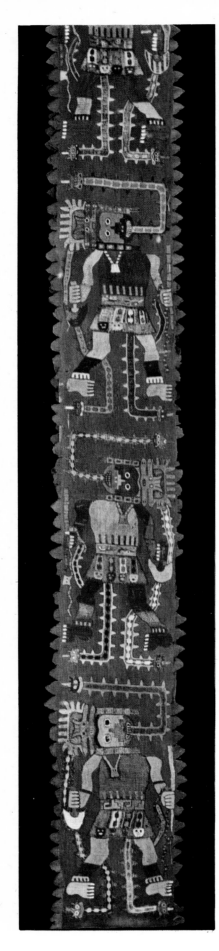

III-4. Paracas woven band decorated with a god and serpents

figures, appear. A new technique, whereby wax was applied to areas of the pottery before painting, was now developed. When the pottery was fired, the wax melted, leaving these areas unpainted.

At this time the Mochicas, a people occupying several of the northern coastal valleys, developed their own fascinating civilization. They made sun-dried adobe bricks of a regular form in molds, and with these bricks they built on a huge scale. But their adobe cities have worn away, and there is little of them to be seen now at ground level. An aerial view, however, can give archeologists some idea of their great earthworks, dams, clusters of houses (which, like the later Incas, they built with pitched roofs), and great stepped pyramids. The largest of these remaining, the Pyramid of the Sun in the Moche Valley, was constructed of 130 million carefully molded

III-6. Paracas fragment of a poncho showing trophy heads

III-7. Paracas textile fragment showing heads of gods

III-8. Paracas textile fragment showing killer whale

bricks. It covers an area measuring 750 by 450 feet, and at one point rises to a height of 135 feet. It is, in fact, the largest single structure in Peru. But unlike the Incas, the Mochicas were primarily worshipers of the moon. This was because they lived on the coast, where the tides were important and the sun all too reliable.

In many other ways, however, the Mochicas were the forebears of the Incas. It was they who first developed an impressive system of irrigation, bringing the water of the rivers to feed broad valleys, and reclaiming deserts by damming and channeling them as they descended. One such mud-lined channel that has been found was no less than eight feet wide, six feet deep, and eighty-seven miles long. It was the Mochicas, too, who seemed to have developed the ayllu, with each village or clan owning its property communally. The Mochica men farmed, fished, and paid their tax by working on public projects. They were ruled by a class of priests, with the assistance of official messengers, warriors, and craftsmen, and such techniques as weaving seem to have been done on a factory scale. Above these were the local chieftains of the valleys, and eventually the rulers of the empire. The farmer population lived in clusters of dwellings at the valley edges (the fertile land of the valley was too valuable to provide living space), while the nobles and their servants occupied walled and terraced hillocks. Here they must have lived in some luxury. Later tales tell of a king surrounded by royal face painters, bathing masters, trumpeters, and feather-weavers.

As among the Incas, laws were strict, and they were stricter for the nobleman than for the common man. But there was a lighter side to life. Children played a form of tennis and badminton, and adults entertained themselves with heavy drinking and watching dancers in elaborate costumes and masks perform to the music of wind and percussion instruments.

You may well ask how we know so much about these long-buried people who had no form of writing yet discovered. We know about them because they recorded every detail of their lives, not in words, but much more vividly in their extraordinary pottery.

These pots were often created in molds

III-9. Mochica effigy vase representing a man with a club

III-10. Mochica effigy vase, probably of a bat god

III-12. Mochica portrait vase

III-11. Mochica portrait vases

(they may even have been mass-produced), and were given a slip, or coating of fine clay, and painted in shades of creamy buff and red before firing. In them we see depicted numerous scenes from Mochica life—soldiers and priests, men playing flutes, women carrying burdens, men masquerading in animal skins, rulers carried in litters. We even see their houses, depicted in every detail, and from these little models we can have a clear idea of Mochica life.

Plates III-9 and III-10 show a Mochica man carrying a club and splendidly dressed in a helmet, handsome ear plugs, and a fine necklace, and one of his gods, in this case a powerful and terrifying bat god. But these are generalized portrayals of a man and a god. In Plates III-11 and III-12 we have something altogether extraordinary. Here we see Mochica features, with high cheekbones, almond eyes, and flaring, hawk-like noses. But these are more than typical faces, they are telling portraits of individual people. They are often rulers or noblemen of importance, shown at different

III-13. Mochica vase in the form of a frog

III-14. Mochica vase depicting a deer with her fawns

periods of their life. These are, in fact, among the first portraits of ancient America, and the finest created before the second millennium A.D. by any people in the world except the Romans. Here we see ancient Mochicas as they actually were, muffled against the evening chill in wool headdresses, wearing their face paint in panels on either side with the middle of the face left unpainted, as was customary among warriors. We do not need writing to tell us that the man at the bottom of Plate III-11 was a sage, and the individual in Plate III-12 a forthright soldier. These figures appear in good health. In other pots we see various maladies and disfigurements—an idiot, an unfortunate with a harelip or disfiguring disease—portrayed with such realism that a modern doctor can diagnose the malady today, at a distance in time of over a thousand years.

III-15. Mochica vase in the form of maize

III-16. Mochica vase depicting a hunting scene

In Mochica pottery we see not only the Mochicas themselves, but the animals with which they lived. Every kind of sea creature is depicted, including the octopus, and every animal, from the jaguar and puma to the duck and the frog, which symbolized moisture. In Plate III-13 we see a frog crouching ready to spring, carefully observed and portrayed with loving attention. Deer must have been a common sight to the Mochicas, as they are portrayed often. Plate III-14 shows us what may be a deer carrying her fawns, or, because of its seemingly human pose (the Mochicas were experts at capturing an animal pose), it may represent a priest disguised in a deerskin.

So taken were the Mochicas with portraying in their pottery the objects of their everyday life that they even portrayed the food they ate, sometimes using real fruits and vegetables to make the molds. The

vase in the form of maize (Plate III-15) was almost certainly made this way. Although, like the Incas, the Mochicas had many kinds of potatoes and beans, maize (corn) was especially important to them. It was eaten fresh off the cob, boiled into a kind of hominy, and cooked with chili-peppers. Popcorn was a favorite delicacy.

Not all Mochica pots took animal, vegetable, or human form. Some were globular in shape, and on their sides were painted scenes from Mochica life. The vase in Plate III-16 combines the two. The scene depicts a hunter, dressed in an elaborate animal headdress, poncho, and skirt, with painted legs and face, in pursuit of a deer shown on the other side of the vase. His weapons consist of a club, arrows, and a spear. Hunting among the Mochicas was an aristocratic sport, and noble hunters were assisted by dogs and beaters who drove the

101

III-17. Mochica vase painted with a figure of a warrior

prey into nets. The deer modeled above the scene probably represents the god of hunting. The hearty figure we see on the vase in Plate III-17 is a warrior, armed with helmet, club, and shield, and wearing a bag which may have been used to carry the heads he cut off in battle.

This pottery gives us a picture of a kind of Homeric society, with petty chieftains fighting each other; of people living vigorously, if not always decorously; and of a people who paid great attention to their appearance, painting their faces and limbs

III-18. Mochica ear ornament of mosaic and gold

and decking themselves out in elaborate clothing and jewelry—ear ornaments, nose plugs, necklaces, and adornments of every sort.

Plate III-18 shows us a finely worked ear ornament made of gold and mosaic, and Plate III-19 a simple and elegant breast ornament with the relief of a feline deity in hammered gold. Gold and other metalwork developed in the first millennium B.C., but the Mochicas brought to it a new excellence. These objects have been found because the Mochicas, like the ancient Egyptians, lavished elaborate burials on their chieftains. With the corpse were placed all the objects he had loved in life, sometimes including his favorite wife (chieftains were polygamous), who might be placed in his arms alive. But with him, too, were placed many pots and vases representing things familiar to him, and serving perhaps the same purpose as tomb wall paintings did in ancient Egypt—to create for the spirit an afterlife like that he had known on earth. It is because of this custom that we have the superb pottery with which we can re-create Mochica life.

The Mochica was not the only culture of the Early Intermediate period. There were, for example, the Nazcas, who lived on the coastal plains to the south. These were a mysterious people, none of whose architecture remains, and about whom little is known, other than that they were descendants of the people of the Paracas culture, and that they left behind them strange "lines," some miles in length, etched into the sands, and sometimes representing huge animals and insects. Like the ruined cities of the Mochicas, these monster-sized expressions are best seen from the air, and there is a theory that they were to be seen in their entirety only by the sky gods. The Nazca people created pottery not nearly so

III-19. Mochica breast ornament in gold

III-20. Late Nazca effigy vase in the form of a seated hunchback

III-21. Monolithic carving from the Gateway of the Sun

III-22. Stone figure

well modeled as the Mochica. In fact, their pots may seem haphazard in shape, like the figure of the seated hunchback in Plate III-20. But, whereas the Mochica potters used only two colors, the Nazca potters used as many as eleven colors on one vessel, and these were altogether decorative and lively.

Suddenly, around 900 A.D., the Mochica empire fell, overthrown by the followers of a new religion. This religion seems to have had its center in the city of Tiahuanaco, near Lake Titicaca high in the Andes, and the city of Huari, near the present Ayacucho. This was the very time that the great cultures of the Classical period of Mexico were overthrown, and there seems to have been, at this moment in history, a great movement of peoples throughout Mexico and Central and South America. In Peru this new period is called the Middle Horizon.

Tiahuanaco, like Chavín before it, was a religious center to which pilgrims came from all over the Andes, and although its power was immense, it was not a city in the usual sense. In fact, its bleak surroundings could have supported little population. Being situated in the hills, it was built of stone, not adobe brick, and a splendid array of its monuments still remains. On the high, barren Altiplano twelve miles from Lake Titicaca itself, are still to be seen the remains of a pyramid that covered an area of 690 feet square and stood 50 feet high, platform-type monuments, stairways, and great monolithic gateways, all faced with huge blocks of finely dressed stone, some 30 feet in width. The most famous of these is the Gateway of the Sun. In Plate III-21 we see the lintel from above this great gate, and we should examine it closely, as it is the key to the art of Tiahuanaco. It is carved in a flat, low relief, which is typical of the style of Tiahuanaco, and the figures have been reduced to an abstract pattern of flat rectangles, very different from the free-flowing, realistic figures of the Mochicas. The god himself stands in the center. Sun's rays leap from his head, and he holds in each hand a staff, decorated with puma and condor heads. Beneath his eyes his cheeks bear markings that might be falcon markings, or even tears. On either side winged figures holding snake-headed staves form a rectangular pattern. The image of this figure, the "weeping god," is stamped everywhere to which the power of Tiahuanaco spread.

Along with the monuments of Tiahuanaco there stand great stone figures like the one in Plate III-22. In the style of the place, the details of the figure are carved in low relief on the cylindrical form of the stone pillar itself, which has kept its original shape. Again the figure is geometric and rigid, and there is nothing of the freely curving elasticity of Mochica sculpture.

The delicate carving on the belt of this statue represents the design of an exquisite textile, and in fact the weaving of Tiahuanaco must have been very fine. Unfortunately, all of these textiles have perished in the damp climate of the highlands, but some examples of weaving in the style of Huari have been found on the coast. The fragment of fabric in the form of a glove in Plate III-23 is such a piece, and again we see the flat, geometric designs of Tiahuanaco. They can be seen, too, in the skull cap decorated with feather mosaic in

III-23. Woven fabric in the form of a glove

III-24. Skull cap ornamented with feather mosaic work

Plate III-24, which gives us some idea of the richness of dress of the period. (Unlike the Mexicans, the Peruvians did not have to keep aviaries to obtain beautifully colored feathers. All such birds flew in the coastal valleys and nearby tropical hills of Peru.) But the designs we see here and on pottery (Plate III-25) seem too busy, too elaborate, and this became a fault with the later style of Huari. Still in some objects, like the superb mosaic mirror in Plate III-26, the geometrical design in delicate colors creates an effect of ethereal beauty.

The forces of Huari seem to have gradually conquered the Nazcas on the southern coast of Peru and obliterated their culture. The arrival of the newcomers can be identified not only by the images of Tiahuanaco and Huari, which are to be found everywhere, but by the habit of building, not with the small adobe bricks usual to the coast, but with huge adobe blocks recalling the large stones of the highlands. The followers of the god of Tiahuanaco seem then to have overthrown one after another of the Mochica cities, until all that was left of the Mochica empire were a few strongholds in the north.

Unlike the Nazca, however, the Mochica culture never died, and when, around 1250 A.D., the power of Huari began to wane, it was a people descended from the Mochicas, the Chimus, who took hold and formed a new empire in the Mochica tradition. These were all coastal kingdoms, overlapping geographically, but not in time. The Chimus encompassed Mochica lands and more—actually different capitals conquered neighboring areas.

But whereas the Mochicas were grouped in small communities, the Chimus lived in well-organized cities. This last great period of civilization in Peru before the arrival of the Spaniards is called the Late Horizon.

III-25. Vase in the Huari style

Everything in the kingdom of Chimor was done on a much larger scale, and craftsmanship suffered as a result. Now there was a demand for mass-produced pots and molds, which the Mochicas had used sparingly, and standard forms replaced the individuality of the extraordinary Mochica vessels. The basic pottery shapes of the Mochicas were continued and double spouts from the south were introduced, but the quality was poor (Plate III-27). Red or brown and cream-colored pots were still made, but by far the most common were the black vessels made in a reducing furnace and burnished, a process which occurred seldom in the earlier period. Now, too, pottery was often decorated with elaborate sculptural relief (Plate III-28).

It has been suggested that these black vessels were made for poor people in imitation of the metal vessels of the nobility. Certainly gold and silver came into use in

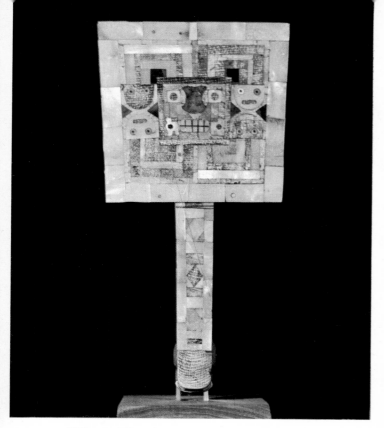

III-26. Mosaic mirror

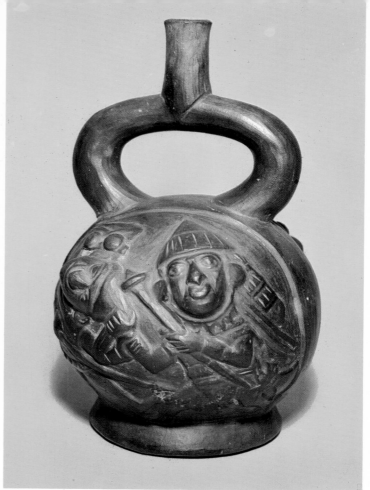

III-28. Vase with relief decoration

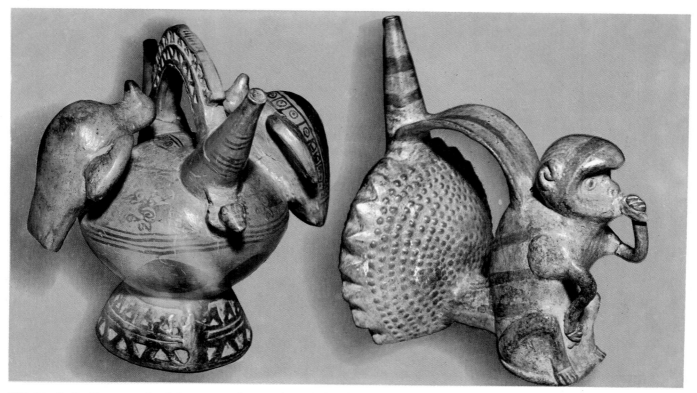

III-27. Left: Pottery double-spouted vessel with birds in relief   Right: Double whistling vase in the form of a monkey

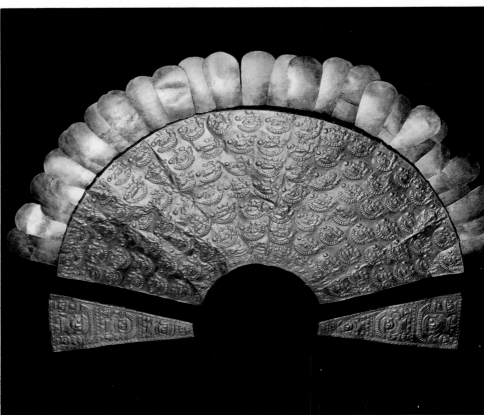

III-29. Gold breast and nose ornaments and necklaces

III-30. Gold breastplate and shoulder straps

vast amounts, the gold for which Peru was later to be famous. Not only jewelry and other bodily adornments (Plates III-29 and III-30), but drinking vessels as well (Plate III-31) were made of these precious metals. So famed for their exquisite work were the Chimu metalsmiths, reproducing the designs of pottery by hammered-out *repoussé* relief, that the Incas later brought their entire metalworkers guild to Cuzco. Meanwhile these objects tell us of the great richness of the kingdom of Chimor.

Chimor was not only rich, it was spectacular. The Chimus elaborated the system of irrigation of the Mochicas, and the cities of the kingdom were linked by twenty-foot-wide roads, protected from the shifting sands of the desert by adobe walls. On them traveled swift messengers in relays, forerunners of the Inca couriers. Their capital, Chan-Chan, was the greatest me-

III-31. Gold bracelet and gold beaker with a human face in relief

tropolis yet seen in South America. It covered an area of eight square miles, divided into four tribal units, and surrounded by a mass of small dwellings. It is thought to have housed fifty thousand souls, with regular streets, gabled houses, and gardens watered by canals. Its huge reservoir held two million cubic feet of water. It is not surprising that this powerful empire of the coast should have come in conflict, in the fifteenth century, with the growing mountain empire of the Incas. Nor is it surprising that when the two finally joined battle in 1461, the luxury-loving Chimus were defeated by the well-disciplined and more puritanical forces from the highlands.

But the Incas were not conquerors to be feared. Once a territory was overcome, they immediately set out with constructive plans to turn it into an active, satisfied part of their empire. Local customs, religions, and language were allowed, but the cult of the sun was established. The chiefs of the area were then sent to Cuzco to become Incas in spirit, and then often sent back to rule their territory. Roads were now put through the new territory, connecting it with the great network of Inca highways, and, as we have seen, clay models of the area were sent to Cuzco so that new and better systems of irrigation could be devised. If the ayllu system did not exist, it was established, and professional architects were sent from Cuzco to plan and build towns of Inca type. Thinly settled regions were populated by Quechua-speaking peoples loyal to the Incas. Above all, foes who offered no resistance were treated with kindness. The Lord-Inca's sentiments were just: "These will soon be our people as much as others."[2] So it was that within two centuries the Incas had created one of

the largest empires in history, an empire so united in language and culture that not even four hundred years of Spanish rule has been able to obliterate its stamp. But, as we have seen, the Incas were the organizers not the creators of their culture.

As artists the Incas were not as inspired or original as the earlier peoples from whom they inherited their styles. Inca pottery was unimaginative. It was mass-produced in a limited number of shapes, generally covered with a pinkish-brown slip and neat repetitive geometrical ornamentation. This may have been derived from textile design, which was also uninspired, although, like pottery, it exhibited extremely good workmanship.

But it was as architects that the Incas, like the Romans, excelled. The basic form of Inca architecture was the simple, gabled fieldstone house, cemented with adobe and thatched, around which stood courtyards (Plates III-32 and III-33). It was from such a basic unit that all the great buildings of the Incas developed, and great they were. The Inca metropolises contained sun temples in the form of truncated pyramids, buildings to house the priests, temples of the sun virgins, who were in a way the nuns of ancient Peru, administrative offices, storehouses, and palaces to receive the Inca, all of gigantic dimensions. The central square of an Inca city might hold fifty thousand people, and each had a fortress to which the people might retreat in time of danger.

Let us take a closer look at this extraordinary architecture. It was created of great blocks of masonry, and the chief decorative elements were niches in trapezoid form (Plate III-34). Doorways, often roofed with one great block, were also in this form, giving the impression of great strength and height (Plate III-35). These

[2] Victor W. Von Hagen, *Realm of the Incas,* New American Library, New York, 1957, p. 203.

III-32 & 33. Terraces and dwellings at Machu Picchu, Peru

III-34. House of the Altar at Machu Picchu, Peru

III-35. Trapezoid doorways at Machu Picchu, Peru

III-36. View of Machu Picchu, Peru

examples are all taken from Machu Picchu, one of the miracles of American archeology.

Little remains of the great metropolis of Cuzco, and at the beginning of this century, only the vaguest idea of the splendor of Inca architecture could be formed by the scanty remains that had been found. Then, in 1911, a discovery was made that was as important to archeology as the discovery of Pompeii: Machu Picchu, an Inca city frozen in time and almost unchanged since antiquity. It is small wonder that it was not found sooner. The Spaniards had no knowledge of it, and the Incas had made no mention of it. Still, there it stood, overgrown by jungle but unchanged for five hundred years.

If we look at a map, we will see that the Urubamba River runs along the east side of the Andes, and beyond it the land slopes down into what becomes, eventually, the dense jungle of the Amazon. Here

there lived fierce tribes, still to be found there today, whom the Incas were never able to conquer. They built, however, a series of fortress-cities as defenses against these tribes all along the steep cliffs of the Urubamba. Machu Picchu (between the peaks of Machu, or "old," Picchu and Huayna, or "new" Picchu) was the farthest of these from Cuzco, and it was definitely a military installation. Unlike other Inca cities, it was heavily walled, and the land it encompassed, although carefully terraced, could not have supported its inhabitants. These, then, were not mere farmers. They were soldiers supported by the state. Still we see here, in the finely constructed palaces, temples, and simpler gabled houses and barracks, all that is typical of Inca construction: fine stone masonry, with no nails or wood other than poles to support the heavily thatched roofs. In Plate III-36 we can get some idea of the splendid situation

III-37. The fortress of Sacsahuaman

III-38. Detail of stonework at Sacsahuaman

of the place. We can see how the dwelling houses are closely grouped around a central square, and how every inch of space is terraced for cultivation. All this careful planning was done in Cuzco, not with pen and paper, which did not exist, but with clay models of the terrain.

Equally impressive is the great fortress of Sacsahuaman (Plates III-37 and III-38), near Cuzco itself. It is calculated that this great fortress, which protected Cuzco from jungle tribes, took some thirty thousand workers seventy years to construct. To the north it presents a fortified wall more than fifteen hundred feet in length, in three tiers with terraces between, in all sixty feet high. It was guarded by two square towers and contained a palace for the Inca, barracks, storage houses, and an excellent stone water-supply system.

Most fascinating are the giant stones themselves. These are not courses of evenly cut rectangular blocks as at Machu Picchu, but their uneven polygonal shape is deliberate. With no continuous joints they offer far greater resistance to the shocks of earthquakes, which are frequent in the area. The largest stones are of course on the bottom, and we notice that, rather than fitting evenly and presenting a smooth surface, these stones appear to bulge out and to fit carelessly. This is a deception. The joints are in fact so tight that there is scarcely a hair's breadth between them. But here at Sacsahuaman (and this is not true of Machu Picchu), the edges have been deliberately beveled. Like the Renaissance princes who "rusticated" the walls of their palaces, the Incas fabricated this roughness to point out the size of the individual huge blocks and add to their appearance of invincible strength.

But how were such great stones, some of them weighing sixty tons, quarried and worked, without the use of draft animals or heavy metal instruments? We face here the same problem that has perplexed the archeologists of ancient Egypt. It is thought that these great limestone blocks were perhaps pried out of quarries by means of wooden wedges swollen with water. They may then have been pulled by sledges on stone rollers and lifted on ramps. The Incas, of course, had various metals to cut these stones and may have used copper chisels, although they appear to have also used age-old stone hammers, axes, and adzes, and possibly abrasives.

We noted before that the walls of the great buildings of Mexico appear to us elaborately decorated with frescoes and reliefs, while those of Peru seem unadorned. Often the doors of these buildings were brightly painted and set with precious stones, and, in the most important, the interior walls were ablaze with plates of solid gold.

The Incas were, in fact, among the greatest gold-workers in history. The Andes were incredibly rich, and as all gold belonged to the Incas, it was taken directly to Cuzco, at a rate of seven million ounces a year. There was, too, a vast quantity of silver, and Inca metallurgy was well advanced. Copper and tin were combined to produce bronze, and this was sometimes plated with gold or silver. What the Inca goldsmiths could do with this wealth amazed even the Spaniards, accustomed to the great goldsmith work of the Renaissance. One conquistador wrote, "In Cuzco they found many statues and images entirely of gold and silver, the complete shape of a woman in natural size, very well wrought, well shaped and hollow. . . ."[3] Another described "many vessels of gold, lobsters of the sort that grow in the sea," and noted that "on other vessels were sculptured all birds and serpents, even spiders and lizards and a sort of beetle . . . carved on the body of the gold."[3] There was enough of this gorgeous treasure for Atahualpa, the last of the Inca princes, to offer the Spaniards a ransom large enough to fill a huge room, twenty-five by fifteen feet, twice over with silver and once with gold. You may wonder why we see none of such works illustrated in these pages. This is because, by decree of the king of Spain, all the gold and silver from the empire of the Incas was melted down for the royal treasury in Seville. The executors of this law were efficient—not one piece remains.

Amazingly, Pizarro, with his tiny army, was able to seize the empire of the Incas just as Cortez had seized the empire of the Aztecs. There were many parallels. Again there was the legend of the white god who had departed by sea and promised to return, in this case the creator god Viracocha. This haunting myth persisted throughout Mexico and Central and South America and confounds archeologists to this day. Had, in fact, some fair-skinned and bearded traveler from Europe or the Near East set foot on these shores, taught the natives what he knew of another world, and then departed again, perhaps in a hopeless effort to return to his homeland?

Again the Spaniards arrived at a time of internal disorder within the empire. For five years civil war had raged between two brothers, Huáscar and the handsome and brilliant Atahualpa, each proclaiming himself Lord-Inca. When the Spaniards arrived at the port of Tumbes, Atahualpa had just defeated his brother and was resting at the sulphur baths of Cajamarca before his coronation. Amazingly enough, so isolated were the empires of Mexico and Peru that the Incas did not even know of the Aztec Empire, much less the fact that it had fallen to white men from the sea ten years before.

Again the Spaniards were more than humanly courageous. Pizarro led his little band over the highest mountains European man had ever seen, through an empire of many millions, armed to destroy them, to find the Lord-Inca himself. Atahualpa let them come, curious to study at first hand these creatures with the bodies of men and the legs of animals (the Incas thought man and horse were one), who carried thunderbolts with them. He believed that they were so few as to be harmless. To Inca knowledge, no aid could come to anyone from the barren sea.

And again the Spaniards succeeded by seizing the person of the ruler himself. The final scene in the history of the Incas is surely one of the strangest in all history.

Pizarro, when he found the Inca, requested a meeting in the central square of Cajamarca itself. The Inca arrived decked in emeralds and seated on a silver and gold litter decorated with plumes and studded with precious stones. He came with thousands of attendants, but unarmed out of courtesy. He was first approached by Pizarro's chaplain, holding a Bible in one hand and a crucifix in the other, who recited a brief history of the Christian faith and requested the Inca to embrace Christianity and become subject to the king of Spain. The flabbergasted monarch's reply is understandable: "'I will be no man's tributary! I am greater than any prince upon earth. Your emperor may be a great prince: I do not doubt it, when I see that he has sent his subjects so far across the waters; and I am willing to hold him as a brother. As for the Pope of whom you speak, he must be crazy to talk of giving away countries which do not belong to him. For my faith,' he continued, 'I will not change it. Your own God, as you say, was put to death by the very men whom he created. But mine,' he concluded, pointing to his deity—then, alas! sinking in glory behind the mountains—'my God still lives in the heavens, and looks down on his children.'"[4]

The Spaniards replied with a burst of cannon fire and a cavalry charge, both mystifying and terrifying to the Incas. There was a terrible slaughter, the person of the Lord-Inca himself was seized, and Inca history, for all intents and purposes, came to an end.

[3] *Ibid.*, p. 153.
[4] *Ibid.*

The Art of Africa

THE EXTRAORDINARY visual variety presented by African primitive art might easily lead the uninitiated viewer to seek an explanation of the puzzling contrasts, or possibly even conflicts, of style he finds facing him. A term more appropriate or accurate than "the uninitiated" could not be found to describe the stranger to African art, for in traditional tribal societies, every object held a special, frequently secret meaning, a meaning most likely known only to the initiate and his fellow tribesmen. Deep spiritual beliefs and elemental fears drove the African tribesman to endow everything around him with specific meanings or powers; it has been said that in Africa art provided the individual with the means of relating himself to the universe through material symbols.

It might also be said that. art for the African has traditionally served as a kind of extended spiritual vocabulary capable of expressing many abstract thoughts and feelings. Collectively, African tribal art spells out an entire cultural encyclopedia. Tribal societies may be most readily identified by the characteristics of their art; indeed, in Africa, art, contrary to the convenient and popular notion, not only knows boundaries, but designates them.

Today, however, the very topic of African tribal history can provoke unhappiness and anger. Swiftly changing societies within the vast continent of Africa, in the headlong rush to achieve modernization, are not necessarily eager to enshrine the traditional values of their ancestors, whose deep religious convictions are now dismissed as mere superstition. To many, the tribe as an institution, with its inflexible, unchang-

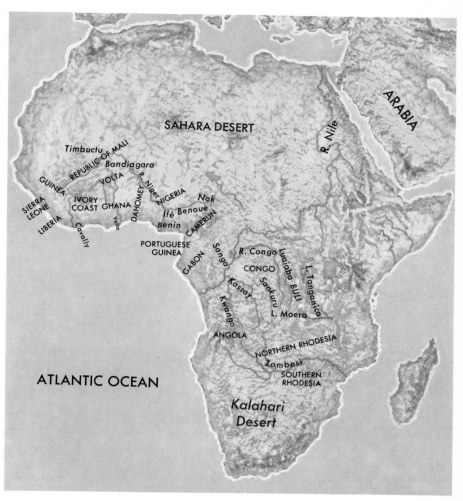

IV-1. Map of African cultural areas

ing patterns of spiritual and physical life, represents a positive menace to contemporary progress and liberated African thoughts. Yet the undeniable fact remains that it has been the tribal societies that have created the major body of African art, which, in this century, has come to be so admired throughout the world.

Many professional Africanists, sociologists, and historians whose lives are spent in the study of Africa are distressed by what they consider the destructive side effects of native antitribal attitudes. Already, in a show of contempt for the past, much traditional tribal art has been lost, either deliberately or by neglect (rot, fire, or termites, under suitable climatic conditions, can make fast work of wood, the African artist's preferred material). On the other hand, much attention has recently been devoted by Africans to the legendary splendors of their vanished kingdoms such as those of ancient Ghana or Songhai. That the courts of these kingdoms sponsored and produced great works is undeniable; however neither magnificence nor grandeur may ever be taken as a binding standard, let alone the single one, when judging art. When speaking of African art, we must therefore bear in mind the crucial differences between court art, which served to glorify and commemorate powerful rulers and ranking nobility, and traditional tribal art, which served to fill the spiritual and social needs of the people.

With few exceptions, the art of each tribe is a separate entity inspired by its religion, philosophy, and traditions, and within itself is always coherent and consistent. The art-producing area of Africa lies within the generally accepted boundaries of the Sahara Desert to the north and the Kalahari Desert to the south, the Great Lakes region to the east and the shores of the Atlantic to the west. No generally accepted explanation however can be offered for the fact that within this sprawling area of West and Central Africa, all or almost all of the tribal sculpture is produced (Plate IV-1). Most probably historical and geographical factors have been responsible. The tribes of West and Central Africa have for the most part remained settled as cultivators of the soil for many centuries, having been discouraged from large-scale migrations both by the impenetrable tropical rain forests of the Congo area, where the sky is obstructed by giant trees that thrive in the steaming mists, and by the terrifyingly parched and desolate eternities of desert wastes hemming them in at the north and south. In East Africa, on the other hand, the pastoral and nomadic peoples look back on a long history of turmoil and conquest, as well as geographically sweeping tribal movements and migrations. The scarcity of sculpture in East Africa may be laid principally to the widespread observance there of the Moslem laws prohibiting graven images.

Actually the earliest known African images are to be found among an estimated fifteen thousand scenes carved and painted on the natural stone walls formed by erosion high on one of the Sahara's central plateaus, called Tassili. Eight thousand years ago, as the Ice Age dwindled in Europe, the Sahara was a lush domain on whose green slopes and winding river banks man hunted the wild animals grazing there. For the next six thousand years, life in the Sahara region was depicted by varying peoples on the hard native rock. In an attempt to clarify and classify the Tassili rock paintings, certain scholars have designated the historical periods of these astounding cultural records as the periods of the Hunter (6000–4000 B.C.), the Herder (4000–1500 B.C.), the Horse (1500–600 B.C.), and ultimately, as the obvious result of calamitous climatic changes, the period of the Camel (600 B.C.–?).

The Tassili rock paintings must be considered unique, however, for elsewhere African tribal art is to be found almost exclusively in sculptural form. The fascinating diversity of African tribal sculpture makes any helpful generalizations practically impossible. However, a brief survey might be offered describing the materials and techniques most frequently used by native artists and craftsmen. In addition, a short list of the most commonly encountered forms of sculpture, such as masks and ancestor figures, could be drawn up, although the significance of each object is less interesting when taken out of tribal context.

Wood carving dominates all other tribal art (that is to say, the visual arts; dancing and drumming are considered by some to represent the supreme achievement, the vibrant soul of African expression). The wood itself may vary widely in its degree of hardness, and it is almost never aged. The tribal wood-carvers, always male, traditionally have preferred to work with living wood and often adapt their designs to take advantage of the tree trunk's natural lines. Tribal wood-carvers seem also to have generally preferred working within the restricted area of a single shaft of wood, and it is for this reason that their sculpture projects such a powerful impression of verticality. Other common traits that can frequently be observed in much tribal art include a seeming disdain for painted surfaces, an equal disinterest in portraying motion, and what the distinguished British authority on African art, William Fagg, has termed "African proportion," in which the figure is presented as being no more than two or three times the length of the head (this customary emphasis on the head, both in elaborated detail and outsized proportion, reflects the African belief that the spirit resides there).

African sculptural techniques may be divided into those of cutting down, the method used in the carving of wood, ivory, and stone; and those of building up, as in the casting of metals and the modeling of pots. The wood-carver's tool is the adze, of which three sizes are generally used for a mask or figure, together with a small sharp knife for finishing the surface. The final polishing of a carving customarily has been assigned to women and children. Clay has been put to many uses in Africa,

and from time to time such diverse materials as shells and feathers, raffia and string, claws and teeth, beads, bones, metals, or even mirrors have been used to heighten the decorative or magical effect of a piece of tribal art. But to discuss such objects in greater detail, we must study African tribal cultures in individual and regional terms.

The Dogon and Bambara of the Sudan

THE HISTORY of the Sudan, written chiefly by Moslem chroniclers, describes a succession of great military kingdoms which at one time achieved an exceptional degree of civilization. The first state to emerge in West Africa, sometime about 600 A.D., was called Ghana. The Sarakolle, the ruling tribe of Ghana, were said to have fought with iron weapons, whereas their less advanced enemies knew only wooden ones. The knowledge of iron apparently had been borne along two routes, one from North Africa to the Niger River, and a second from the middle Nile to Lake Chad. North African conquerors overran Ghana after 1070 and again in the thirteenth century, and the state became converted to Islam. The empire of Mali, under Moslem rule, succeeded Ghana and flourished most brilliantly in the thirteenth and fourteenth centuries. Timbuktu, Mali's principal city, became renowned as a magnificent center of Moslem culture complete with a great Islamic university and many fine mosques.

A fourteenth-century Egyptian chronicler, Ibn Fadl Allah al Omari, described the splendors of the empire of Mali and its ruler: "He is the most important of the Moslem Negro Kings, his land is the largest, his army the most numerous; he is the king who is the most powerful, the richest and most fortunate, the most feared by his enemies and the most able to do good to those around him . . . the region of Mali is that where the residence of the king is situated, in the town of Niane, and all the other regions are dependent on it; it has the official name of Mali because it is the capital of this Kingdom which also includes towns, villages and centers of population to the number of fourteen."

The ancestors of the neighboring Dogon, although geographically isolated on steep cliff-sided plateaus, somehow managed to survive in this forbidding terrain by cultivating crops and by breeding animals to trade with the Moslems in the city of Timbuktu. According to some historians, the Dogon themselves claim to have arrived in their present territory only three or four hundred years ago; they insist that before them, their land was occupied by the so-called Tellem, and to this tribe, they attribute some of their own most ancient artistic relics.

As with other tribal arts of West Africa, the art of the Dogon constitutes a universe of its own. The French Africanist Marcel Griaule, in a study of the relatively modest Dogon civilization, has compiled a list of several thousand of their symbols, substantiating fellow Africanist Georges Balandier's remarks on the subject of characteristic tribal thought in his book *Ambiguous Africa, Cultures in Collision* ". . . everything is attributed to the will of God or the ancestors . . . among these people every object and every social event has a symbolic as well as utilitarian function. It serves and signifies at the same time. Many material creations—houses and granaries, household objects, chairs, receive the impress of symbolic thought, so that the latter is called to mind at all times and in all places. Traditional African societies have not recorded their knowledge in libraries and on monuments; they have registered it in the objects which form the material framework of existence." Actions, too, are assigned symbolic meanings, and as Balandier observes, "the rite is still associated with the tool. This is true whether we are speaking of agricultural techniques and the practices pertaining to fertility, or preindustrial techniques like the art of the forge or the quarrying of gold which assign an important role to ritual."

Of all West African tribes, the Sudanese Dogon are perhaps the least influenced by others; and although some Moslem elements may be detected in their costumes and architecture, they managed to escape the unifying flood of Islam which swept through these parts of Africa a thousand years ago. Their art is the most geometrical and abstract to be created by any West African tribe. The best of their sculptures have great majesty and serenity; their angular, geometric forms being both tightly conventional and strangely arresting in their abstract power. Figures carved with rigidly raised arms are common, especially in the early Dogon works, and appear on doors, food troughs, stools, shutters, and locks. Conventionalized figures of horsemen reflect the Dogon's enthusiasm for riding and are found frequently along with stylized carvings of animals, most probably goats.

A variety of Dogon works appear in Plates IV-2 through IV-9. The characteristic position of the arms, the hands raised up to the heavens with flatly opened palms, is seen in a wooden statue in Plate IV-2. The exact significance of this dramatic gesture is not known, but it possibly

IV-3. Wooden statue with raised arms

IV-2. Statue with raised arms

IV-4. Wooden statue with raised arms

IV-5. Wooden figure astride animal

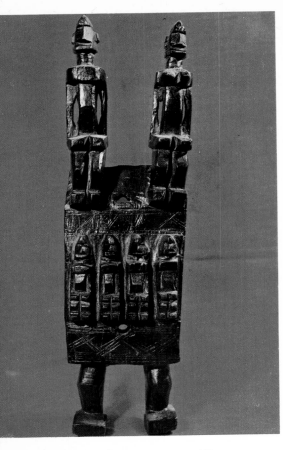

IV-6. Wooden lock with figures

IV-7. Wooden door of a granary

IV-10. Priest's wooden headrest

IV-8. Wooden statue of an ancestor

represents an invocation to the gods for rain. Whatever its religious meaning, this posture is artistically interesting in that it accents the vertical movement of the carving and the intensity of expression in the head, a most important characteristic in all African works. Three similar figures are shown in Plates IV-3, IV-4, and IV-5, the last appearing astride an animal.

On the lock and granary door in Plates IV-6 and IV-7, figures, probably of illustrious ancestors, have been represented. Ancestor figures, such as shown in Plate IV-8, were carved by African tribesmen as sanctuaries for the spirits of their dead relations. These figures did not have to realistically resemble their inhabitants; the soul of a dead man would understand precisely which figure was intended for him and would reside there until final departure for the hereafter. Another purpose of an ancestor figure was to force the spirit to remain in a specific place rather than roam about a village causing trouble and misfortune. As in other African sculpture, ancestor figures are sometimes given both male and female characteristics in the belief, shared by the Dogon, that the separation between the sexes is not absolute.

Ancestral figures were tended with devotion and might be talked to, fed, bathed, or ritualistically anointed with palm oil or other substances; this last attentive gesture frequently resulted in the eventual creation of a distinctive patina, or rich surface texture. Indeed, one of the most important characteristics of Dogon art is the smoothly crusty patina of its wooden statues; the patina of a four-headed figure in Plate IV-9 has been achieved by applications of a Dogon mixture of cooked millet and blood. Other interesting examples of Dogon artistry, a priest's wooden headrest and a dance mask surmounted by a monkey, appear in Plates IV-10 and IV-11.

The Bambara

THE ART of the Bambara, like that of the Dogon, possesses the powerful simplicity characteristic of these subdesert regions. More populous than the Dogon, the Bambara live in western Mali; their religion places even greater emphasis on agriculture and animal fertility, and as a consequence, so does their art. The most famous of all Bambara sculptures are the *Chi Wara,* the stylized antelope headdresses. Composed of a basketwork cap onto which is fastened a highly abstract sculpture of one or more antelopes (Plates IV-12 to IV-14), the Chi Wara is worn in rites reenacting the origins of agriculture. Chi Wara was a mythical ancestor of the Bambara who taught them to sow grain and whose exploits are recalled in ritual dances (the Bambara believe that their divine ancestor lives in a place known only to the antelopes, and that he can assume their long-horned shape at will). These beautiful and imaginative carvings are often decorated with earrings and beads and ironwork and are worn in agricultural plays and dances in which the spirit of Chi Wara is called upon to ensure the fertility of fields and livestock. In Chi Wara antelopes of the horizontal type (Plate IV-13), the head is usually carved separately from the body because of the grain of the wood. In some of the Chi Wara a small figure of a man or an animal is placed on the animal's back or between its horns.

In Bambara spirit masks, anthropomorphic and zoomorphic elements, meaning, respectively, human and animal shapes, are so freely combined, as in the case of Plate IV-15, that it becomes extremely difficult, not to say impossible, to identify the real subject. Bambara artists have created

IV-12. Chi Wara, wooden antelope headdress

IV-9. Wooden four-headed figurine

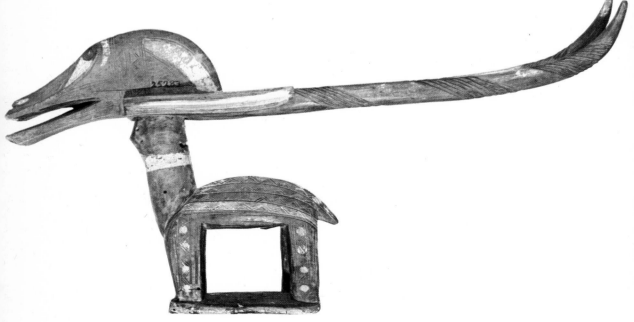

IV-13. Chi Wara of horizontal type

IV-11. Mask surmounted by a monkey

IV-14. Chi Wara of vertical type

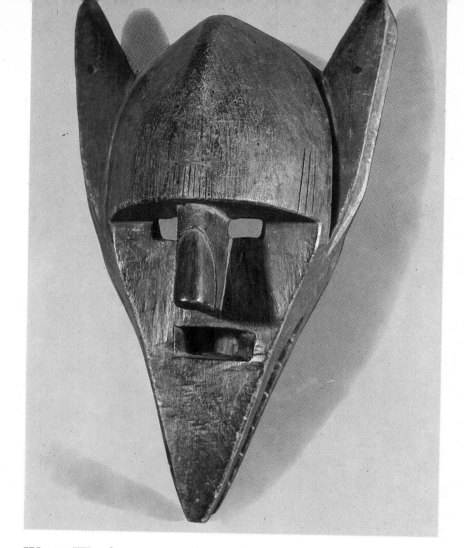

IV-15. Wooden zoomorphic mask

masks and stylized figures of the finest quality (Plates IV-15 to IV-18). Their anthropomorphic statues are severely geometric in style. The Bambara have also produced numerous carvings of heads, or marionettes, with stick bodies draped in geometrically patterned cloth, which were probably used in a kind of puppet play.

Bambara iron sculpture (sculptors also serve as village blacksmiths) is represented by a type of pointed scepter which is thrust into the ground. These scepters are surmounted by masterfully forged representations of human beings, often mounted on horses, and are supposedly used as em-

IV-16. Mask with crocodile

123

IV-17. Wooden mask decorated with cowrie shells

IV-18. Hyena mask

blems of rank among chiefs and elders of the tribe.

A small subtribe of the Bambara is called the Marka. Their style of carving closely resembles that of their neighbors, but their masks differ notably in that they are decorated with a thin copper plating which partly or entirely covers them.

The Mossi, Kurumba, and Bobo

THE ART of the Mossi, the principal tribe of the Voltaic Republic, is distinguished by its fascinating masks. Those of the Wango secret society are composed of two entirely different sections; the lower part being a highly abstracted head surmounted by the upper part, a naturalistically carved figure (Plate IV-20). These towering masks are carved from single pieces of wood and are painted with reddish-brown and dull white colors made from the juices of tree roots and from white clay.

In the region of Tribindi in Mali, the Kurumba have developed a particular style of sculpture, usually representing a long-necked and long-horned antelope which is at the same time both sturdy and graceful (Plate IV-19). They are painted in black, yellow ocher, and blue, with occasional touches of rust red. The older examples are often very beautiful.

The Bobo, who live mostly in Upper Volta, owe their artistic fame to their startlingly tall masks, which, although they are far more fantastic, borrow some characteristics from the Mossi and the Dogon. Vividly painted, their designs are said to be taken from tribal heraldic devices (Plates IV-21 and IV-22). The Bobo-Fing subtribe,

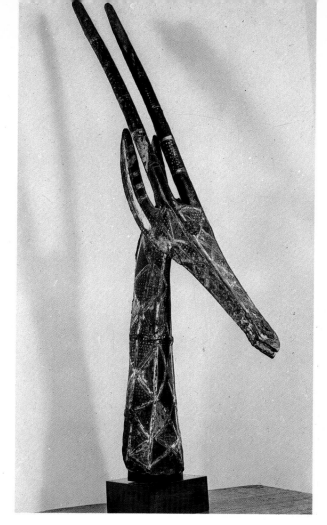

IV-19. Head of an antelope in wood

IV-21. Two masks in painted wood

IV-20. Wooden mask with figure

IV-22. Ritual mask

The Senufo

THE HIGH DRY grassland, called savannah, which covers the northern part of the Ivory Coast, as well as part of Mali and Upper Volta, is the home of the Senufo. The Senufo are peaceful farmers, and their secret men's societies, the Poro and Lo, are a stabilizing force in their culture. Their sculpture, though influenced by the Dogon and Bambara in the north, shows closer relationship to the Guro and Baulé in the south. But in spite of these influences, Senufo sculpture possesses a strong character of its own.

Most of the boldly executed Senufo figure carvings are variations on the same theme, the representation of the ancestor, sometimes feminine, sometimes masculine. The *déblé* figures of the Senufo, often called rhythm pounders, have massive cylindrical bases which are thumped against the ground during certain religious dance ceremonies to solicit the aid of Senufo fertility gods. The severe, elongated female figures have great angular power with their pointed chins, breasts, and bellies and sharply flexed knees (Plates IV-23 and IV-24). So too do the numerous Senufo statuettes of men on horseback.

The so-called fire-spitter masks (Plate IV-25) are important to the Gbon cult of the Senufo and show an extraordinary synthesis, or blending, of animal and human features. In the Korubla secret society, an antiwitchcraft cult, the same type of grotesque human-animal masks are used "to chase witches." Another form of large, abstract helmet mask (Plate IV-26), topped

which lives around the town of Bobo-Dioulasso, also produces an elegant form of ovoid, or egg-shaped, helmet mask in hardwood, often surmounted by naturalistic human figures. An example of such a Bobo-Fing mask, in which the features show a certain fidelity to anatomical reality, appears in Plate IV-22. When worn by a dancer, the shaggy raffia beard would cover most of his upper body, thereby creating the wonderfully eerie effect of a floating figure from another world.

IV-23. Deblé or "rhythm pounder"

IV-24. Statue of a woman in wood

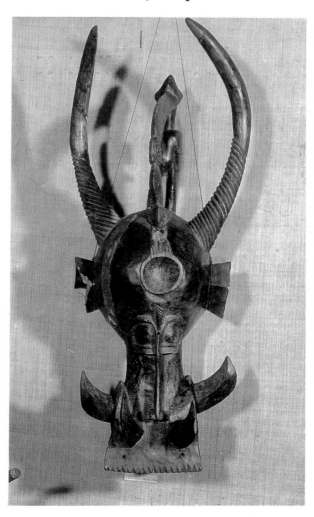

IV-25. Wooden fire-spitter mask

IV-26. Two-headed animal helmet mask

with birds and figures and sometimes heavily horned, is called *degele*. The hornbill, a bird often seen and heard in that part of Africa, is one of the favorite totemic animals of the Senufo. It is frequently seen together with the tortoise, the crocodile, the chameleon, and the snake in the artistic decoration of many objects such as large drums and the decorative doors of cult houses. The hornbill sometimes appears by itself, in greatly magnified form, as a guardian of Senufo villages.

Guinean Art

From Senegal south to Angola, the life of the people is dominated by the dense coastal rain forest interspersed occasionally, as in Ghana and Liberia, with wedges of dry savannah country. While the rainy climate creates conditions of rampaging fertility, it also complicates communication between the various tribes; as a consequence, tribes with highly developed cultures often live close to others less advanced and neither see them or even know of their existence.

The art of the Republic of Guinea is best represented in the Baga tribe, whose most significant contribution to African primitive art is the massive Nimba (the great spirit of fertility) masks, sculptured in a very hard and heavy greenish-gray wood (Plates IV-27 to IV-30). These stylized female busts are characterized by rounded shoulders and full, elongated breasts (see Plate IV-29). The Nimba figures are carved with heads of unusual, jutting proportions decorated with welts and complicated scarifications, a form of raised, three-dimensional tattooing popular with many African tribes. The great hooked nose and the tiny button-like mouth over a small pointed chin are also characteristic features. These masks are carried on the shoulders of a dancer in the course of ritual ceremonies of the Nimba cult; a long raffia cloak hides the dancer, who is able to peer out from holes between the breasts.

The most interesting feature of the Baga drum in Plate IV-30 is the supporting base composed of four Nimba statuettes, recognizable by their hooked profiles. Yet, while the Nimba head is certainly the most recurrent motif in Baga sculpture, it is by no means the only theme. In Plate IV-31, for

IV-27. Head of a Nimba mask

IV-28. Nimba figure

IV-29. Nimba bust

IV-30. Drum with Nimba figures

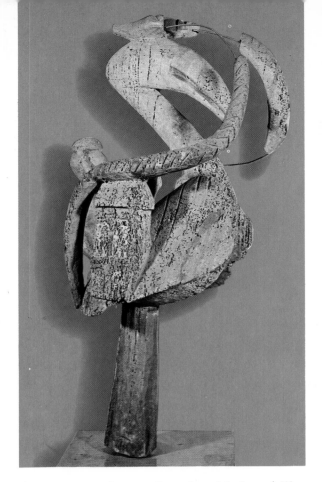

IV-31. Carved top of mask with hornbill

IV-32. Soapstone statuette

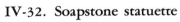

IV-33. Anthropomorphic stone statue

130

IV-34. Nomoli soapstone figure

IV-35. Man's head in soapstone

example, the mask reproduced is of a hornbill with long curving neck and beak.

In the interior of Guinea, and the nearby parts of Sierra Leone, are found ancient soapstone figures called *pomdo* by the Kissi, whose ancestors probably made them within the last few centuries. They are still used in divination today (Plates IV-32 and IV-33). Related to both these Kissi pomdo and Baga sculpture are the soapstone *nomoli* made centuries ago by the Sherbro of Sierra Leone (Plates IV-34 and IV-35).

The Art of the Ivory Coast

The western part of the Ivory Coast and its neighboring territories of Liberia and Guinea are dominated by the extremely powerful Poro-like secret organizations. The influence exerted by the Poro is extended by the trade and exchange system among the tribes under its sway, the Dan and their associated tribes, the Kran, the Man, the Gio, the Geh, the Ngere, and also the Kono of Guinea.

A single Ivory Coast artist will often create an entire range of mask styles, from naturalistic portraits to grotesque abstractions. The typical Dan mask in its pure form (Plate IV-36) is oval and naturalistically simple. Highly polished to a warm glowing brown, the eyes are either shown as mere slits (female) or, as in this case, as great staring circles (male). To these masks there is often added a hair beard or moustache, and in both male and female masks, the coiffure, of braided fiber or grass, is attached through small holes bored into the wood.

The Ngere, called the Kran in Liberia, live south and west of the Dan. The Ngere sculptural style is abstractly expressive (Plates IV-37 and IV-38), and by using horns or tubular projections for eyes and

IV-36. Wooden mask

IV-38. Wooden antelope mask

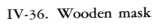

IV-37. Two wooden masks

cheekbones, an atmosphere of fear and menace is created.

The Guro tribe live in the central part of the Ivory Coast and, like the Dan-Ngere tribes, specialize almost exclusively in masks, which usually present a combination of animal and human features. A beautiful Guro antelope mask appears in Plate IV-38. One minor but exquisite aspect of Guro art is the decoration on the pulleys on their looms, depicting small heads of animals or humans. These probably represent spirits who keep watch over the weaving.

The Baulé

The populous group called the Baulé live to the east of the Guro and south of the Senufo near the central area of the Ivory Coast. Following severe dynastic controversy with their Ashanti brothers sometime about 1730, the Baulé migrated from the Gold Coast bringing with them the arts of casting. Wood sculpture only really developed among the Baulé after they had come in contact with the Guro and Senufo, and had begun to evolve a kingdom of their own. They proved to be superb carvers as well as metalsmiths, with a style notable for its calm elegance and mysterious charm.

The chief characteristics of a Baulé figure carving (see Plates IV-39 and IV-40) are the slender rounded body with decorative weals (raised scar tissue); delicately carved fingernails; oversized head in proportion to the body; high forehead; arched brows; heavy-lidded, protruding eyes; straight nose with flattened nostrils; small mouth; and beautifully arranged hair (on male statues, small braided beards), the entire sculpture being carefully smoothed, darkened, and sometimes rubbed with oil. Baulé masks are glowingly serene and look like benign

IV-39. Wooden female figure

133

IV-40. Wooden figure of a woman wearing bead ornaments

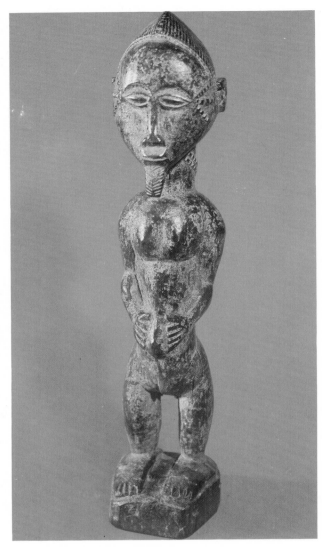

IV-41. Wooden figure of a woman

phantoms; they are usually human in aspect, although on occasion are zoomorphic as in the large bovine masks of Guli, the buffalo spirit. Meticulous attention is paid to such details as individual's hairs, the precise geometric scarifications called *cicatrices,* and the luxurious sheen of the sculpture's surface (Plates IV-39 to IV-42).

Gbekre, the god who judges the dead, is represented in an almost savagely gro-

tesque manner by Baulé carvers. He appears as a saber-toothed, baboon-headed monster of a man with huge flat feet. In his hands he invariably holds a bowl or cup, probably for ceremonial offerings (Plate IV-43).

The Baulé's decorative art includes the skilled carving of doors, stools, and drums (Plate IV-44); their little loom pulleys have the same fanciful charm as those of the

IV-42. Wooden mask

IV-44. Sculptured drum

IV-43. Gbekre, the monkey god

Guro. Perhaps the most captivating arti-
fact produced by the Baulé is the mouse
oracle (Plate IV-45), a round-lidded box, in
this instance attached to a contemplative
male figure. Straws are placed in the box
in a prescribed pattern by a medicine man
who then recites a few incantations as a
mouse is released from a lower chamber to
scramble about among the straws. The
disturbed straws are then read to foretell the
future or answer personal questions.

135

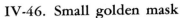
IV-45. Mouse-oracle box

IV-46. Small golden mask

IV-47. Gold jewel

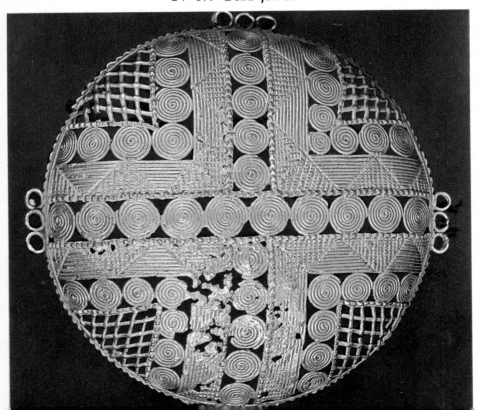

Implements used in Baulé ceremonial rituals, such as fly whisks, batons, and sword handles, were also carved in wood and then covered with gleaming gold. Gold was and still is cast by the Baulé—small human masks, beads, rings, crocodiles, decorative discs, and other ornamental shapes (Plates IV-46 and IV-47). These precious objects are not for everyday use but are reserved for chiefs and for the Gold Festival, which every other year ensures the survival and fertility of the tribe.

The Ashanti

The Akan-speaking peoples make up one of the most important groups of African art-producing tribes. In turn, the greatest of these Akan states is that of the Ashanti, the dreaded "forest warriors" of the nineteenth century who live in the former British colony of the Gold Coast, now named Ghana. The Gold Coast derived its name from the fact that the area boasts some of the world's richest gold mines. The primary Ashanti political unit is the village, governed by a council of elders "equally composed of old men and old women of wisdom." The village headman is elected for life but can be abruptly removed by the elders if he loses their confidence. A state, or *oman,* is formed by a number of loosely linked villages and is ruled by a chief or minor king (*omanhene*) and his elders, whose government is a slightly more complex version of that of the village. Within each state, a single clan provides the royal lineage and candidates, the omanhene being nominated by the queen mother of this clan upon the death of the chief.

The chief or king traditionally has been said to be the personal representative of the sun, and gold, symbol of the sun, was his monopoly. The Ashanti's strong supernatural associations with gold reach back to sometime around 1700 when the Ashanti state of Kumasi was ruled by a certain Osei Tutu, who had a great adviser, a medicine man named Anokye. It was Anokye who united the Ashanti federation of states as the result of a miracle, a heavenly apparition. It is said that Osei Tutu, at that time simply an omanhene, was peacefully settled upon his official seat when suddenly his attention was drawn by Anokye to a wondrous shining gold stool floating from Heaven. To Osei Tutu's happy surprise, it came crashing down upon his knees. This indeed was a sign from God, declared Anokye, that henceforth Osei Tutu should be recognized as king of kings, or *asantehene,* and he sent word to all the chiefs of the land to come to Kumasi and prostrate themselves before their divinely appointed ruler; this they did, and swore a binding blood oath that they would preserve the golden stool, which enshrined the *sunsum,* or soul, of all the Ashanti people, as well as pledging eternal allegiance to the asantehene.

Ashanti art has been increasingly dominated by gold during the last few centuries and there is surprisingly little wood sculpture, apart from the little dolls called *a'kua'ba* (Plate IV-48), which are worn tucked in the small of the back of women to assure the birth of a handsome child.

IV-48. An a'kua'ba doll

IV-49. Soul-washer's badges

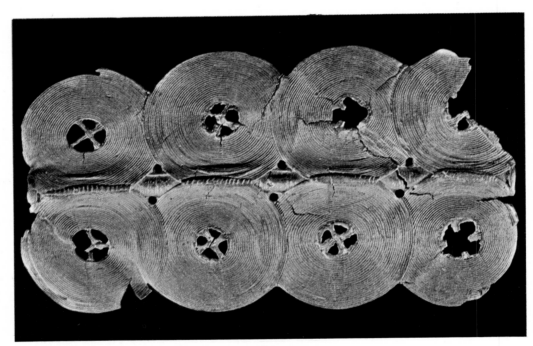

IV-50. Elaborate gold bead from necklace

The excellent quality of Ashanti goldwork is particularly remarkable for its delicacy, as may be seen in Plates IV-49 and IV-50, badges of the king's "soul-washers" and a fragment of an elaborate necklace. That a Near Eastern influence may be detected in these pieces is possibly explained by the fact that Ashanti territories are not restricted solely to the impenetrable rain forests but extend well into a wedge of dry savannah that permits relatively easy contact with the east.

The Yoruba

Of all the new African nations, only in Nigeria can the mainstream of art history be followed for over two thousand years. The most important elements of Nigerian art are the sculptures of the ancient Yoruba tribe, of the kingdom of Benin, and of the recently-discovered Nok culture.

The Yoruba, a large tribe of more than ten million people, have produced far more sculpture than any other tribe in Africa. Most of it, such as shrine figures and furniture and masks for cult dances, was designed for religious purposes. The Yoruba live mainly in the southwestern area of Nigeria and traditionally have been organized into city-states ruled over by divine kings, each of these kings governing his own hierarchy, or ranking scale of major and minor chiefs. For at least two thousand years the Yoruba have possessed a cultural unity under their divine kings, who in their turn have looked up to their spiritual leader, the Oni of Ife. The onis of Ife were descended from the mythical Odudua, the founder of the dynasty and one of the gods sent down from heaven to supervise creation of the earth.

The stylistic uniformity of Yoruba art is easily recognizable. The masks for the Gelede or Egungun societies, the huge *Epa* helmet masks, the human figures for religious shrines and the small *ibeji,* figures of twins, each have an identifiable style. All the Yoruba secret societies, religious cults dedicated to the well-being and betterment of their members, used a distinctive type of mask in their dances, plays, and ceremonies. Those of the Gelede and Egungun societies (Plates IV-51 and IV-52) are somewhat alike; they are worn on top of the head, their pierced eyes serving no other purpose than to lend a more life-like ap-

IV-51. Gelede mask

IV-52. Wooden mask

IV-53. Epa mask   IV-54. Ivory horseman   IV-55. Woman suckling a child

pearance to the mask. The Epa mask in Plate IV-53, carved from a single piece of wood, represents a warrior on horseback (*jagunjagun*) with an attendant seen in "social perspective," that is to say that the warrior's height and the small size of the horse and the attendant are meant to symbolize their relative importance in society. The ivory horseman in Plate IV-54 was made for the Ogboni society, a cult devoted to the appeasement of earth spirits; in his hands are held *edan Ogboni,* ritual brass heads cast on iron rods.

The wooden figure of a woman suckling a child, seen in Plate IV-55, is carved from *iroko* wood, soft when cut fresh for carving, yet hard enough to resist termites when dry. Surmounting her head is the double-axe symbol of Shango, the thunder god. In Plate IV-56 we find a wooden statuette of a twin. Throughout Yorubaland, when a twin dies, a wood-carver is called upon to carve *ibeji,* twin figures, for the cult devoted to their care and memory, so that the second twin does not follow the first. These small wooden figures are always of the same size and posture, although they differ in hair styles, exterior decoration, and the personal style of the individual artist. When a twin dies, the surviving twin is held responsible for the tending of the ibeji, which is kept in the family shrine, and seeing to its ceremonial washing and feeding; if both twins are dead, this duty falls to the family.

IV-56. Statuette of a twin

The Ife Heads

For centuries the sacred city of the Yoruba has been Ife, on the edge of the tropical rain forest. It was there, in 1910, that the German Africanist Leo Frobenius first discovered the bronze and terra-cotta masterpieces of some unknown artists of the thirteenth century (Plates IV-57, IV-58, IV-59). So extraordinarily beautiful are these sculptures in both technique and form that it seemed at first incredible that they should be the works of artists native to such an inaccessibly remote tropical area. For a short time, German archeologists even toyed with the idea that they might be relics from the legendary lost continent of Atlantis. Now the celebrated bronze heads of Ife are usually considered the greatest achievements of African art, with a classical beauty and nobility comparable only to the finest Greek and Renaissance sculpture. To date, about twenty bronze heads have been found, as well as many terra-cottas and bronze castings varying from stools to small groups of human beings.

It is thought probable that all the famous heads are portraits of divine kings, the *onis* of Ife, or at least of men of great authority, such as chiefs or priests of the city. In any case, this is court art at its finest; a departure from the almost complete naturalism of the Ife sculptures is found only in the idealized modeling of the ears or in the occasional stylized rings around the neck (Plates IV-60, IV-61). It is interesting to note that the only full-length bronze figure so far to have been found, a portrait of an oni of Ife elaborately dressed in heavy necklaces and bracelets, a draped sarong, and an ornamental head-dress, again has been given what Africanist William Fagg terms the "African proportion," that is to say that, in height, the sturdy, compact body measures only slightly more than twice the length of the head; this is of vital importance as it obviously disproves certain improbable theories that the sculptors of Ife had had knowledge of or contact with classical European artistic techniques and traditions.

A number of artists must have worked in the holy city of Ife for many years, and certainly their skill in *cire perdue,* lost-wax, casting has never been excelled. Some of the heads measure only about one-sixteenth of an inch in thickness. Incidentally, even today the Ashanti make charming little golden ornaments by what could be called the lost-beetle, rather than lost-wax, process; a beetle is buried in a small ball of clay, a miniature spout is inserted to the center, the clay is baked, reducing the beetle to ash, the ashes are flushed out, and molten gold is poured into the cavity left by the recently departed occupant. When the clay is chipped away, a precisely realistic golden beetle emerges from the core.

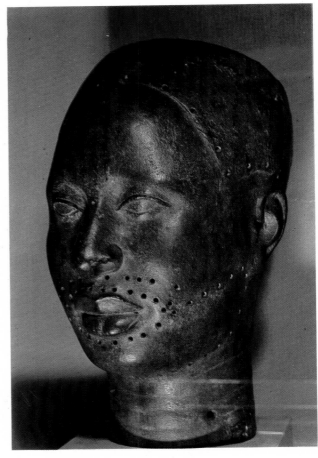

IV-58. Portrait head of a king

IV-59. Head of a king

IV-57. Bronze head of a king (oni)

IV-60. Bust in bronze

IV-61. Terra-cotta head

The Sculpture of Benin

The ancient kingdom of Benin, unexpectedly located a little more than a hundred miles from Ife, in the midst of a steaming tropical rain forest, is famous for its court bronzes. Before the discovery of the Ife bronzes, the Benin sculptures served as the only historical evidence we had of West Africa's artistic past. The sculptural style of Benin, which probably derived from the Ife court tradition sometime towards the close of the fourteenth century, was intended to glorify and commemorate the ruling *oba,* or king, and his court. Except in the very early bronzes such as the portrait head of a queen mother shown in Plate IV-62, Benin bronzework is overshadowed today by the classical beauty of the Ife sculpture, the reason for this being its gradual degeneration due to the court's vain preoccupation with imperial pomp.

In Plate IV-63, a bronze plaque depicts the oba in full regalia, brandishing a ceremonial sword and spear and attended by a musician, a bearer, and two warriors with shields. Hundreds of plaques like this were nailed to the square wooden posts supporting the shingled roofs of the courtyard gallery in the palace of the oba of Benin in the seventeenth century, the middle period of Benin art history. Cast by the *cire perdue* method, the plaques exalted the oba and members of his court and household, always in "social perspective," and served the purpose of recording the history of royal military campaigns and other memorable exploits; in Plate IV-64 the oba is shown riding sidesaddle in a procession, resplendent in headdress and ornaments of heavy coral beads, the Benin court status stone, and maintaining his regal balance with the aid of two attentive guards.

Heavy coral necklaces like neck braces are worn by the tusk-crowned oba in Plate

IV-62. Portrait head of a queen mother

IV-64. Oba riding in procession

IV-63. Bronze plaque

IV-65. Head of an oba with tusk

IV-66. Ivory scepter with captain on horseback

IV-65, and by a war captain on horseback surmounting an ivory scepter in Plate IV-66. When a hunter, member of one of the most respected social strata of Benin society, felled an elephant, one tusk had automatically to be presented as a gift to the oba; sometimes the gift would be incorporated in a portrait of the oba and the sculpture would be displayed upon the altar of the royal family.

The oba held a monopoly on bronze, and its use was strictly limited to the environs of the court. For this reason, the art of the Bini, simple tribal inhabitants of the oba's kingdom, mostly consisted of carvings in wood, ivory, and terra cotta (Plate IV-67).

The ancient arts of Ife and Benin may well be derived from the much earlier Nok culture of northern Nigeria, which was identified less than thirty years ago through sculptural relics discovered in the tin mines in the country of the Ham or Jaba tribe. (Bernard Fagg, Africanist and brother of William, chose "Nok" as a generic name after a Jaba village about a hundred miles southwest of Jos.) The pieces discovered so far (Plate IV-68) have been dated by

IV-67. Terra-cotta vase with seated woman

IV-68. Ancient head in terra cotta

archeological carbon tests and other scientific methods to the period between the fifth century B.C. and the second century A.D. The Nok terra-cottas indicate an association with both iron tools and polished stone axes, suggesting that the Iron Age was in the process of replacing the Neolithic.

The most outstanding finds have been heads of great intensity of expression in style and conception. They make it clear that Nok sculptors, while working in a stylized manner, at times produced very naturalistic works. Obviously the hundreds of terra-cotta heads and other fragments of pottery so far discovered cannot be assumed to be the earliest examples of an artistic tradition; there must have been antecedents, probably either of wood or unfired clay, for many centuries before.

In the wide area in which the various Nok sculptures have been found, there now live many small tribes, all speaking different languages, and many of them have produced excellent works of art, such as masks, and ancestor or guardian figures, although they are rare and difficult to find compared with those of southern Nigeria.

The Ijo

Ijo art is noted for the simplicity and forcefulness of its water-spirit masks. The Ijo also made great funeral shrines for the tombs of society chiefs from woven reeds lashed together, and to which were fastened jointed wooden seated figures, powerfully simplified and more than half life-size. The highly stylized figure in Plate IV-69 is an *ejiri,* or "soul protector." The sharply jutting angles of the figure and the boldly geometric planes, characteristic of Ijo art, are both astonishingly "modern" and intensely expressive.

IV-70. Wooden figure pounding grain

IV-71. Painted wooden mask

IV-69. An ejiri, or "soul protector"

The Ibo

A large eastern Nigerian tribe, the Ibo are known for their various dance societies and so-called secret societies that employ a great variety of sculptural styles in making ritual artifacts (Plate IV-70). The Mmwo society, for example, create somewhat naturalistic helmet masks, usually with ghostly white faces, to represent the spirits of dead virgins. *Ikenga* are carvings made as personal shrines dedicated to the power of a man's right hand. Fine stools from the western Ibo are also greatly admired, as are their wooden bowls and boxes.

The Ibibio

Living to the east and south of the Ibo are their neighbors the Ibibio. The Ibibio make characteristic masks for their dance societies that are painted brightly in black, white, and yellow. The mask in Plate IV-71 is typical of the Ibibio style with its distinctive tribal marks above the nose and in front of the ears. The Ibibio also carved large wooden figures with jointed arms before which human sacrifices used to be performed; these figures, along with smaller replicas of them, were called "mothers of ghosts."

The ancestor figures of the Oron, a group who are generally included in the Ibibio, but whose carvings bear no relation to those of their cousins, are among the most impressive yet to be found in Africa.

IV-72. Skin-covered dance headdress

IV-73. Seated man. Ekoi

The Ekoi

The naturalistic style of the Ekoi carved heads, often covered with antelope skin and crowned with imposing curled horns, is easily recognizable (Plate IV-72), the carved heads sometimes being used as headdresses in certain funeral rites. The open-mouthed speaking expression is repeated in a more geometrically carved figure of a seated man in Plate IV-73.

The Cameroons Grasslands

The art of the Cameroons is well known from the large quantities of Bamum and Bamiléké work dispersed throughout the world. Bamiléké shapes are freer than those of almost any other tribe and their masks, figures, and stools show a preference for simple, naturalistic forms. Their work is not polished and smoothed after being hewn with an adze, giving it a strongly masculine appeal (Plate IV-74).

The Bamiléké also show a taste for sculptures of their chiefs, and are fond of decorating their palaces and cult houses with decoratively wrought posts completely covered with carved figures of humans and animals (Plate IV-75). A king's throne in Plate IV-76 represents a chief with two of his wives forming the back of the chair. Supporting the seat, carved in one piece from seat to base, is a row of human figures and animals including elephant heads and an elongated leopard. Leopards play an important role in Bamiléké folk tales and proverbs, and in sculpture they appear frequently on the bases of stools and beds. Elephants also are popular with Cameroons craftsmen, and one sees them as helmet masks, as small brass pipes, and as handles for large bowls for palm wine.

The tribes of the Cameroons grasslands are more or less interdependent. Some make splendid stools, while others excel in brasswork or in the creation of fanciful pottery pipes. Cameroons artists are frequently adept at complicated beadwork; sometimes whole thrones have been covered with intricately beaded figures. Other grasslands tribes noted for their original and spirited work are the Bikom, the Bafum, the Bamessing, the Bangwa, and the Bacham.

IV-75. Carved wooden doorframe

IV-74. Wooden mask

IV-76. King's throne

IV-77. Figure of a man in wood

IV-78. Head on elongated neck

The Fang of Gaboon

The third great region of sculpture-producing Africa encompasses the great basin of humid equatorial forest and savannah drained by the Congo and its many tributaries. The group of tribes called the Fang (in French, the Pahouin, and in German, the Pangwe), once the most ferocious warriors on the continent, number over a million and live in Gabon, a territory bordered by the former French Cameroons to the north, the Spanish colony of Río Muni and the Atlantic Ocean to the west, and the former province of Moyen Congo to the east and south. Their most famous works of art, guardian effigies called *bieri* (Plate IV-77), are fastened to cylindrically shaped receptacles made of basketry or tree bark in which are reverently deposited

IV-79. Dance mask

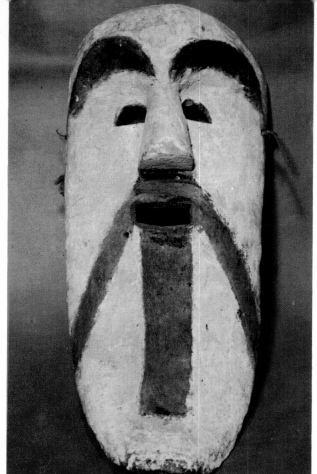

IV-80. Dance mask in wood

IV-81. Heart-shaped dance mask

the skulls, small bones, and other relics of deceased ancestors. The bieri have fairly naturalistic rounded bodies in the characteristic African proportion, with large heads, long torsos, and short legs in proportion to the body. The eyes, made of metal discs or bone, are usually set deeply in hollows and the chin projects to balance the high, bulging forehead. The bieri figures are almost always seated on long wooden "tails" or props which fit snugly into or over the bark boxes that hold the skulls. Often merely the heads, perched on extremely long necks, are carved for bieri (Plate IV-78).

Besides the guardian figures for ancestral reliquaries, the Fang also designed highly expressive masks (Plates IV-79 and IV-80). The Fang and the neighboring Bakwele like to carve heart-shaped faces such as seen in Plate IV-81 (a habit of many tribal sculptors, in the Pacific Islands as well as in Africa). These are often used in ceremonial funeral dances, and are painted white, the color of death in these regions of Africa.

The Bakwele and the Bakota

The Bakwele and the Bakota, whose masks somewhat resemble those of the Fang, are two important tribes of Gabon and of the nearby Congo Republic (Brazzaville). Aside from their heart-shaped face masks, the Bakwele also make cylindrical dance helmets, painted white and with faces carved on four sides.

The funerary figures of the Bakota, made of wood to which thin strips and sheets of brass and copper are fastened, serve exactly the same purpose as the bieri, the guardian figures of the Fang, except that, in the case of the Bakota, the skulls and bones of distinguished ancestors are kept in open baskets in which also rest the lozenge-shaped bodies of the guardian figures. Completely abstract in design, these brass- and copper-

IV-82. Anthropomorphic figure

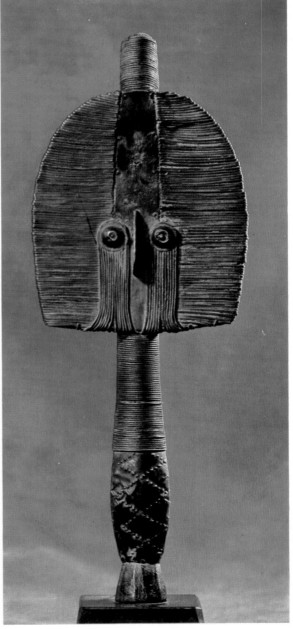

IV-83. Reliquary figure

152

plated guardian figures (Plate IV-82) have great flat faces. There is a substyle of the Bakota in which both sides of the concave and fan-shaped head are metal-plated; these sculptures are quite rare and have been tentatively named Osyeba; the lozenge which fits into the skull basket of these so-called Osyeba figures is carved at right angles to the big head encased in fine metal strips (Plate IV-83).

The remarkable contrast between the forms of the guardian figures among the neighboring Fang and Bakota tribes (and again among the Ambete just to the south of the Bakota) strikingly demonstrates the almost infinite sculptural variety created by peoples of the same type and environment in Africa. The Fang carvers, for example, fully exploited the possibilities presented by sculpture in the round and brought to it a sense of deep human feeling; the Bakota, on the other hand, with equally dramatic effect produced fascinatingly original and abstract low-relief sculpture. It was no doubt for this reason that Bakota figures were among the first African forms to be translated into the terms of modern European painting, principally in Picasso's "Les Demoiselles d'Avignon" of 1907.

The Balumbo

The Balumbo live between the Mpongwe and Ogowe rivers and are members of an extensive complex of tribes whose religious beliefs and secret societies are similar to those of the Fang and the Bakota. Beautiful dance masks with white faces and brown coiffures are made by their carvers for members of the Mukui secret society, who use such masks (Plate IV-84) for funeral celebrations and dances in which the dancers sometimes perform on tall stilts. The sensitive oval faces of these

IV-84. Spirit mask

masks, representing the souls of dead women, with their delicate high-arched brows, slit eyes, and formal coiffures, bear a striking resemblance to some Oriental works of art.

The Bakongo

The Bakongo are a large tribe spread over much of the western portion of the Congo River basin. Their sculpture is more naturalistic than most tribal art, a fact that some Africanists attribute to the Bakongo's close contact with Europeans for more than 450 years. Statues of female ancestors (Plates IV-85 and IV-86), often gracefully seated on crossed legs and balancing babies on their knees, are particularly characteristic of

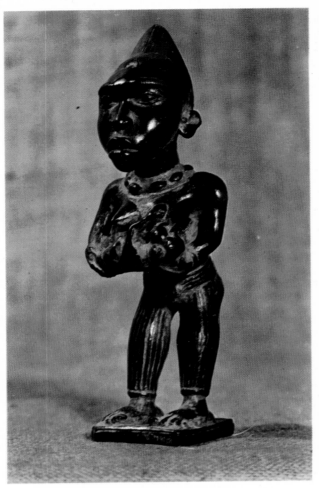

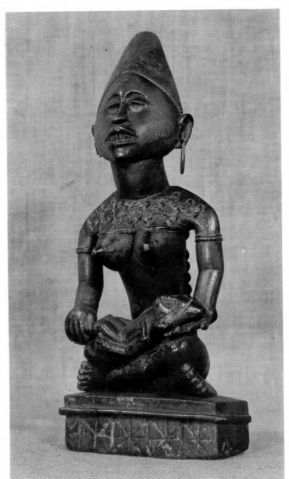

IV-85 & 86. Ancestor statues in wood

Bakongo tribal art. Bakongo ancestor sculpture is widely appreciated in the West for its dignity and grace; the Bakongo are among the few tribes to carve ancestor figures in stone, as the soft steatite (soapstone) available to them can be easily modeled in the same style as the wooden ancestor figures (Plate IV-87).

Even today, as in the past, the fetish plays an important part in the religious life of the western Congo tribes. A fetish can be any object used to evoke magical powers. The *konde* or "nail fetish," peculiar to the Bakongo tribe, is among the strangest to be found anywhere. The konde is a "machine" for direct control of supernatural forces and does not represent a person or a spirit. When the fetish is not covered with nails, its overall form appears quite crude and unnaturalistic (Plate

IV-88). In this example, a skirt of raffia, a few feathers, two iron belts, and some scraps of leather around the waist and chin add to the barbarous appearance of the fetish. To activate the fetish and bring forth its powers, a medicine man drives a nail, knife, or some other piece of iron into the fetish each time he needs its assistance. Sometimes after years of use the original sculpture almost disappears from view, lost in a menacing thicket of nails and iron blades as the fetish in Plate IV-89.

The Bayaka and the Bapende

The Bayaka live in the region between the Kwango and the Inzia rivers, two southern tributaries of the Kasai, which is, in its turn, one of the great tributaries of the Congo River. The Bayaka are fervent believers in fetishes, "medicines" and magic spells. They are also well known for their particular style of helmet mask; when the young men of the tribe return from the "bush university" where they are prepared

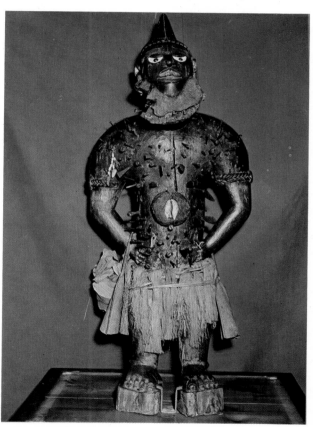

IV-88. Nail fetish

IV-89. Nail fetish

IV-90. Painted dance mask with raffia beard IV-91. Wooden figure of a drummer

for their initiation into the tribe as adults, dances are performed in which such masks are worn (Plate IV-90). Great dance festivals are held in the home villages of the boys, and prizes are awarded for the most original masks. The masks are usually designed with a carved wooden face beneath a superstructure of wood and fiber, all fastened to a bushy cap of raffia or other fibers which covers the entire head of the dancer. The body of the dancing boy is hidden by a very full short cloak of cloth and fiber fastened around the neck. The *nganga,* or medicine man, in charge of the ritual initiation wears a huge mask.

The characteristic sculptural style of the Bayaka is easily identifiable by the exagger-

atedly turned up nose, the large protruding ears, the bulging eyes, and the curving hairline which encircles the upper part of the face (Plate IV-91).

Equally distinctive masks are made by the Bapende, a tribe who live a little to the east of the Bayaka. Typical features of their initiation masks are the converging eyebrows (Plate IV-92), high rounded forehead, drooping eyelids, short nose, and prominent teeth. After the Bapende circumcision rites, the young male initiates are permitted to wear small ivory pendant masks representing themselves in their previous "dead" state, since they believe they are reborn following the rites of circumcision.

The solemnly dignified figure of a regal mother holding a child and a symbolic axe in Plate IV-93 once adorned the rooftop of a Bapende chief; the axe represents the chief's supreme power. Figures similar to this traditionally loomed over the entrances of royal Bapende houses; this example is a valuable rarity, as very few have been preserved.

The Bakuba

Not far from the Bapende, in the region between the Kasai and Sankuru rivers, live the Bakuba, sometimes known as the Bu-shongo. The Bakuba's elaborate historical tradition dates back to long before the era of their great King Shamba Bolongongo (*c.* 1600), who reputedly instituted the custom of having a portrait statue of the king carved during his lifetime. Bakuba royal portraits were invariably carved in the same cross-legged position and were traditionally placed by the pillow of the king's successor so that the new ruler might absorb the wisdom of the old. In Plate IV-94 is shown the statue of Kwete Kata Mbula, the 109th of the Bakuba dynasty, who ruled at

IV-93. Figure of a woman and child

IV-92. Wooden initiation mask

IV-94. Statue of Kwete Kata Mbula

IV-95. Statue of Kwete Peshanga Kena

IV-96. Dance mask

the beginning of the last century; a more recent royal portrait statue, of Kwete Peshanga Kena, who ruled from approximately 1900 until 1918, appears in Plate IV-95. All such sculptures sit on a characteristic pedestal, in this case ornamented with geometric carvings in low relief.

A great deal of Bakuba art, including the royal statues, seems to be derived from the ancient kingdom of Kongo, one of whose kings, as depicted in a Dutch engraving of 1642, received prostrated delegations of European delegates beneath an imported brass chandelier. It is sometimes said that there are two kinds of Bakuba art, one representing the style of the king's court and the other, "the popular style." However, the only objects one could categorize as "court art" are the royal portraits, for in daily life, courtiers and tribesmen alike made use of the same carved boxes for rouge (powdered camwood), razors, and jewels, and they drank and ate from the same carved bowls, cups, and beakers. The decorative patterns of these various artifacts are centuries old, and all hold a deep significance for the Bakuba.

Bakuba dance masks, such as that shown in Plate IV-96, have been carved until very recently. They are sometimes copper-covered, or made of cloth or basketry, with only the nose and mouth separately carved in wood; the elaborate trimmings include beads, bright paint, strips of cloth and leather, and cowrie shells, the last having been used for centuries as a form of money by African tribesmen. The Bakuba are famous, too, for their raffia embroidered cloths, and, in fact, the characteristic geometric patterns of their wood carving (as can be seen in the royal portraits) probably were inspired by textile patterns introduced in the sixteenth century from the kingdom of Kongo.

The Bena Lulua

The comparatively small Bena Lulua tribe live to the south of the Bakuba on the river Lulua, yet another of the southern tributaries of the Congo. While the Bena Lulua have to some extent been influenced by the Bakuba in their way of life, their art retains an unmistakable character of its own. Bena Lulua carved figures (Plates IV-97, IV-98, and IV-99), unlike, let us say, the Bakuba royal portraits, do not invite the touch. To the contrary, for all their intricate curves and roundnesses, they seem to bristle with unexpected sharp

IV-97. Woman and child

IV-98. Figure of a chief

IV-100. Fetish

IV-99. Figure of a girl

edges and protrusions. Undeniably elegant, these small Bena Lulua figures, probably representing chiefs and queen mothers, are characterized by the ornamental scarifications on their heads and bodies, especially around the navel and the joints, and by their somewhat irritated-looking eyes, their complicated coiffures and pointed headdresses, their long slender necks, delicate noses, and strangely pursed lips.

Many Bena Lulua carvings taper to a point forming a spike which is thrust into the ground in front of houses. These are guardian figures whose responsibility it is to protect an owner's property and to ensure his personal safety while he is away hunting. Squatting figures with elbows resting on the knees are sometimes carved as snuff mortars, or, if they are made on a larger scale, as prized fetishes (Plate IV-100).

The Baluba

The Baluba, a large complex of tribes, occupy vast territories in the southeastern area of the Congo, where, a few hundred years ago, they were united in a powerful military confederation. Baluba ancestor figures are among the most handsome in all Africa. The swelling curves of human flesh seem to have inspired the line and form of Baluba sculpture; other characteristics include a certain mild serenity of expression—oval faces with sleepy eyes, rigidly arranged hair, decorative cicatrices or scarifications; the whole is enhanced by a richly glowing patina. Sometimes actual horns and snail shells are added to Baluba sculptures to emphasize the beauty of natural curving lines.

A lovely Baluba maiden supports a stool in Plate IV-101; this carving captures the very essence of femininity and youthful grace, and like other familiar everyday Baluba artifacts, such as headrests and food bowls, is complete in itself as a work of art. The delicate headrest in Plate IV-102 is supported by two almost identical girls with traditional coiffures built up over wickerwork foundations and bodies sculpted in African proportion; the entire sculpture, like that in Plate IV-103, has been lovingly smoothed to a satiny patina through the course of many years. Baluba headrests were specifically designed to keep elaborate coiffures, such as those worn by the girls, clear of the ground or the bed during sleep.

The Baluba were an aggressive tribe, and

IV-101. Wooden stool

IV-102. Headrest

IV-103. Wooden bowl

IV-104. Arrow holder

during the period of confederation, some centuries ago, succeeded in absorbing within their territorial limits a large number of other tribes who more or less adopted the Baluba forms of art. The arrows of a great chief once rested upon the trident supported by a female figure in Plate IV-104, and during certain ceremonies it was thrust into the ground as a symbol of his power.

The Basonge

The Basonge, in some ways related to both the Baluba and the Bakuba, are one of the larger tribes of the Congo and live between the Lualaba and the Sankuru rivers. In sculpture, the Basonge prefer sharp angles and contrasting forms, and their fetishes are charged with an almost ferocious force (Plate IV-105). Their

masks are dramatically abstract, calling to mind modern European cubist sculpture (Plates IV-105 and IV-106); they are said to be particularly impressive and moving when seen in the motion of the dance.

Basonge carved figures have great feet that seem made to grip the earth, and splay-fingered hands spanning round bellies into which large doses of "medicine," concocted by medicine men from gums, excrement, bits of reptiles, and blood, have been ritually poured. Horns filled with this medicine, which was not meant for human consumption but to activate spirits, often topped the heads of fetishes (Plate IV-107); and strings of small wooden figures, shells, beads, drinking horns, and such were strung around their middles.

Interesting stools are made by the Basonge, sturdy enough to hold the great

IV-105. Dance mask

IV-107. Fetish

IV-106. Dance mask

weight, considered suitable to his rank, of even the heaviest chief. Their customary design, that of a man or woman supporting the seat of the stool on their fingertips, dates back to the days when chiefs are said to have sat on the heads or the bowed backs of their slaves.

The Bajokwe

The Bajokwe tribe are spread over the southeastern Congo and Angola in widely separated communities. The characteristic style of the Bajokwe sculpture is distinguished primarily by the "bespectacled" eyes, as seen in the figure of a seated man in Plate IV-108. Other typical features are the elaborately constructed coiffures or "bonnets," exaggeratedly large, and realistically carved, hands and feet.

Bojokwe art is strongly influenced by

IV-108. Seated man

IV-109. Tobacco mortar

both the Baluba and the Lunda, but the forms are less gentle and more massive than Baluba sculpture. The same gleaming, finely polished patina, however, is to be seen in tobacco mortars and seats upheld by caryatids, the classical Greek term for female figures used as architectural supports (Plates IV-109 and IV-110).

The Balega

The Balega are a little-known people of artistic importance living in the southern part of Kivu province in the Republic of Congo. They are governed by the Bwami, a religious and social society to which every Balega man and woman belongs. The

IV-110. Seat supported by caryatids

Kindi, the highest rank of the Bwami society, which dominates Balega life to the exclusion of all else, use sculptures of ivory and elephant bone in their ceremonies; these carvings have a great simplicity as well as a kind of pathetic grace (Plates IV-111 and IV-112).

Figures and masks of ivory, bone, and soapstone can only be owned and used by the Kindi; those of wood are used by the Yanami, the second highest rank. The carvings, be they masks or figures, serve many functions and are assigned many symbolic meanings, such as rank or special power, and they are all associated with hundreds of proverbs expressing the Bwami society's social values and known only to its members.

IV-111. Ivory mask

IV-112. Anthropomorphic figure in ivory

The Art of Australia and Oceania

By the term "Oceania," we mean the islands of the Pacific lying to the east of Indonesia, Malaysia, and the Philippines. Apart from most of Australia, much of the land of this area lies within the tropics, and although the many islands of Oceania are separated by hundreds and sometimes thousands of miles of sea, there are overall cultural similarities to be found throughout the entire area.

The islands differ greatly from the continent of Australia, from New Zealand, and from each other. They vary in size and conformation from New Guinea, which is about fifteen hundred miles long and has

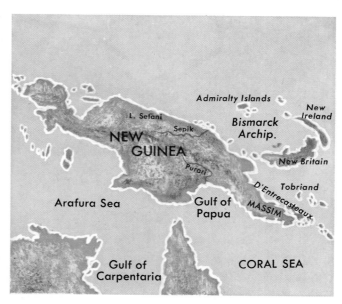

V-2. Map of New Guinea

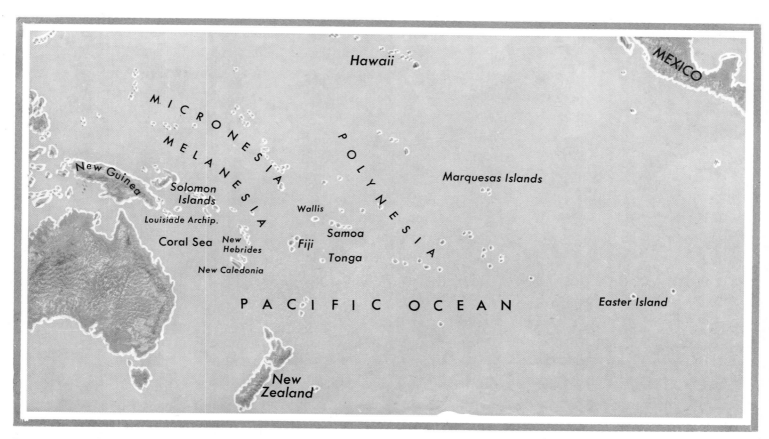

V-1. Map of Oceanic cultural areas

mountains rising over sixteen thousand feet, to minute coral atolls only a few feet above sea level. Many are covered with thick tropical forests, some of the densest in the world, and they were populated by successive waves of immigration from the Asian land mass over a period of several thousand years.

The islands are grouped, along cultural lines, into three main divisions (Plate V-1). Melanesia, in the western Pacific, includes New Guinea (Plate V-2) and other large islands as well as many coral islets. Polynesia includes the islands of the central and eastern Pacific, some of which are high and fertile, while others are low and relatively poor. The Polynesians also colonized New Zealand. In Micronesia, to the northwest, the islands are small and scattered, and have few natural resources. Generally speaking, the peoples of Melanesia and Australia are dark-skinned, with crinkly hair, while those of Micronesia and Polynesia are lighter-skinned, with wavy or straight hair. But none of these divisions are clear-cut. The history of the peopling of the Pacific has been a long and complicated one, and cultural frontiers are blurred.

At the time that the first Europeans arrived in the South Seas, the peoples of Australia and the Islands were at the cultural level to be found in Europe during the New Stone Age. Their cutting tools were made of ground stone or shell, and while some subsisted on settled gardening, others were mere food gatherers, moving from area to area in search of plants and game. Many relied on the riches of the sea.

As in most of the primitive societies we have seen, everyday objects were usually made and decorated by the user. More important undertakings, such as the carving of canoe ornaments, were often reserved for specialists, who possessed not only technical skills, but a knowledge of the rites that would impart magical power to the object. Often such artists, like those of the Sepik River region of New Guinea, were among the most highly respected members of the tribe.

Above all, art was bound up with religion. The general forms of religion—totemism, animism, and ancestor worship—which we have found in other primitive societies are to be found here, along with ceremonies of singing, masked dancing to simple musical instruments, and the telling of legendary tales. But beliefs varied widely from area to area. Melanesian religion, for example, consisted largely in the propitiation and control of the spirits of objects and natural phenomena by magical means. The Polynesians, on the other hand, believed in an elaborate pantheon of great gods, rather like those of ancient Greece, who presided over departments of human life, like war and craftsmanship, and personified elemental forces. Their chiefs were considered to be descended from these gods, and their mythology included a story of the beginning of the world. But everywhere, as in many primitive societies throughout the world, it was felt that works of art had magical properties. In the words of Erwin O. Christensen, "A decorated drum had a better sound than a plain drum, an arrow engraved with an eye ornament had a more certain aim, a face or figure at the end of a spear representing its spirit guided the spear to its destination."[5]

Art in such societies is conservative—little change is expected or allowed. The figure an artist carves is not meant to represent the inspiration of an individual artist, but what the changeless spirits or ghosts of the invisible world are thought

[5]Erwin O. Christensen, *Primitive Art*, Thomas Y. Crowell, New York, 1955, p. 267.

to actually resemble. Still, a general development does occur. In Melanesia, for example, masks and carvings which play an essential part in rituals are discarded after each celebration and are made afresh for the next one. Under these circumstances, changes in style must eventually take place. In Polynesia, artistic objects, often carved from hardwood or stone, are more permanent. Yet here, too, there is an evolution.

Sculpture in wood is the art form for which Oceania is most famous. Stone is used locally, but is much less common. In Melanesia, patterns are painted on sheets of bark or palm spathe. Barkcloth is decorated in colors by various methods in both Melanesia and Polynesia, and in Melanesia it is used for covering masks. The most commonly used pigments are red and yellow ocher; white is obtained by burning shells or crushing limestone; black from soot. All are mixed with water or fat, and various other vegetable and mineral dyes are known. For carving (before the introduction of steel tools), stone, bone, or shell-bladed adzes or axes, chert or obsidian flakes, teeth and bone gouges were used; for painting, the finger or the frayed end of a stick. Jewelry and body ornaments were made of shells, feathers, and human hair.

Using these simple materials, the peoples of Australia and Oceania made ancestral figures, ceremonial objects, carefully decorated weapons, and household utensils. But not all such objects existed in every area. For example, pottery is found only in New Guinea, and rock painting in New Guinea and Australia. Metalwork and large-scale stone architecture are scarcely to be found at all. The inhabitants of each area created what suited them best with the materials they had at hand. A closer look at their art will give us some idea of the

V-3. Ceremonial stool

great variety of their objects and ornamental motifs.

Melanesia is tremendously rich in art, and there are a vast number of local styles, probably due to lack of communication—the terrain of the larger islands is difficult, and unlike the Polynesians, the Melanesians are not good sailors. Sculpture in the round, usually made of wood and often brilliantly painted with schematic patterns, is found throughout Melanesia. If we look at some of these figures, we can form an idea of the great variety of styles.

In Plate V-3 we see a ceremonial stool from the Sepik River region of New Guinea. This area produces a wealth of superbly painted masks, figures, house-posts, shields, charms, and canoe prows—considered the finest in the entire area of the South Seas. The ceremonial stools, generally attached to the figure of a man which forms the back, were not used as actual seats by living men. Rather they were seats of ancestor spirits who thus symbolically attended debates. The figure, a haunting vision, is painted and tattooed as the ancestor himself might have decorated his body, and the white eyes peering from their black shadows give the figure a terrifying, all too real presence. The smoothly finished ancestor figure from the Santa Cruz group in the Solomon Islands (Plate V-4) has a similar realism of bodily form. But the face is generalized into a geometric pattern, and it inspires no such fear. Compared with these, the ancestor figure from the West Irian area of New Guinea (Plate V-5) seems stylized—the human figure has disintegrated and its elements have been rearranged into a formal pattern. The spirit figure from the Gulf of Papua (Plate V-6) is totally stylized, and carved in relief on the flat surface of the figure. Yet its spindly, geometrically bent limbs suggest the

V-4. Ancestor figure

nervous intensity to be found in all Melanesian art.

Most interesting of all, perhaps, is the Malanggan carving from New Ireland (Plate V-7), one gloriously abstract composition. These carvings are made in connection with ceremonies held at intervals in honor of those who have died since the previous celebration and which are also the occasion for the initiation of boys. They represent ancestral and other spirits and mythical beings, and the carvers are specialists. The right to have a certain pattern

V-5. Ancestor figure

V-6. Wood figure representing a spirit

V-8. Figure from the supporting post of a chief's house

V-7. Malanggan carving

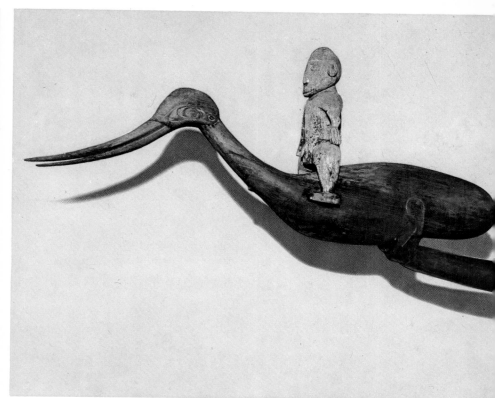

V-10. Wood roof finial in the form of a duck

V-9. Upper portion of a central post, probably of a cult house

made is possessed by certain individuals and is transferable. However, the carver has some freedom, and since the carvings are discarded after each ceremony, there is considerable variation. This use of three-dimensional openwork with the feeling for enclosed space is not to be found elsewhere in Oceanic art. The lavish use of color is equaled only in a few other parts of Melanesia, and it usually bears little relation to sculptural form.

The figure holding a child and composed of delicately carved curves in Plate V-8, also from West Irian, from Lake Sentani, was probably the top of a supporting post of a chief's house. Many of the wooden architectural parts of important houses (generally made of thatch and leaves) were elaborately decorated. The vivid face with flaring nostrils and protruding tongue in Plate V-9, from the Sepik River region, was

V-11. **Wood rigging block of a canoe**

V-13. **Blade of a paddle**

also the upper portion of a central post, probably of a cult house. The charming duck in Plate V-10 was a roof finial. Parts of ships were also carved. In Plate V-11 we see the wood rigging block of a canoe decorated with a human figure, and in Plate V-12, the carved wood ornament from the prow of a boat. These are probably ancestor figures, and their purpose is to provide magical protection. The blade of a paddle from the Solomon Islands (Plate V-13) is elegantly painted with black and red pigment. All these are excellent examples of the adaptation of human or animal forms to practical purposes and the overall design of useful objects.

Wooden shields, too, were often elaborately carved in relief and painted. In Plate V-14 we see a shield from the West Irian region of New Guinea, in which the elements of the human body have been re-

V-12. **Carved wood ornament from the prow of a canoe**

arranged into a formal pattern. Flat paintings are also to be found in Melanesia. In Plate V-15 we see a splendid wild-eyed abstraction, painted in red, white, and black on sheets of sago palm-leaf sheaths, from a cult house in the Sepik River region.

One way in which Melanesian art differed from Polynesian art was in the creation and use of masks. These represent spirits, and were usually worn with long fringes or skirts of leaves so that the body of the wearer was concealed. Women and children often believed that these masks were in fact spirits, and the wearers themselves, although aware of the deception, felt a mystical identification with the spirits they represented during the ecstatic ceremonies at which they were worn.

Like the masks of the Indians of North America and the tribesmen of Africa, the faces of these masks reflect images from the human unconscious. The mask from the Sepik River in Plate V-16, its contours elaborately picked out with swirling linear decoration, has all the nervous intensity we see again and again in Melanesian art. This is even truer of the tortured and twisted visage painted on a barkcloth mask from New Britain (Plate V-17). The mask of tree-fern wood decorated with boar's tusk, from New Hebrides, exhibits a strange beauty in the deep blue of its paint and finely wrought decoration (Plate V-18). Perhaps most frightening is the mask from the Sepik River in Plate V-19. In the words of Sir Herbert Read, "We cannot, in our art, recreate such primitive magic, but in looking at these . . . we may still feel some tremor, along our nerves, of a primeval terror."

The art of Polynesia is much less varied than that of Melanesia. In most of the islands the great gods were represented by idols, stylized in various ways, but usually

V-14. Shield

V-15. Painting on sheets of sago palm-leaf sheaths

V-16. Mask representing the founder of a clan

V-17. Mask of painted barkcloth

V-18. Mask of tree-fern wood

in recognizable human form. In Tahiti, however, the main deities were curiously represented by blocks of wood covered with closely plaited coconut fiber and red feathers, the faces and limbs merely indicated by applied cords; and in the Cook Islands, by enormous lengths of barkcloth rolled on carved staffs, or by conventionalized stone adzes, which represented a craftsman's god.

Yet there were more realistic Tahitian wooden figures which portrayed minor spirits and which were the "familiars" of sorcerers. The Hawaiians, too, made solid, muscular wooden figures, like that in Plate V-20, representing a deity with a tall headdress carved in elaborate openwork. The Hawaiians often portrayed their gods with ferocious, scowling faces, and this is particularly true of the large heads covered with red feathers, made on a base of net stretched over a wicker frame, which represented the war god Kukailimoku and were carried into battle. These could be eight feet tall, and they were meant to frighten the enemy. We can only wonder at the terrifying beauty of these fiery objects (Plate V-21). Few of them are left, however. Most were destroyed in the mid-nineteenth century when King Kamehameha II of Hawaii was converted to Christianity.

Like the Indians of Mexico and South America, the Hawaiian chieftains made cloaks and capes out of brilliant feathers attached to net. The Hawaiians were also experts at making barkcloth. This they

V-20. Wood figure of a deity

V-19. Mask of painted wood

V-21. Head of the war god Kukaili-moku

V-22. Barkcloth

V-24. Ivory female figure

V-25. Wood figure of an ancestor

V-23. Figure of the great god Tangaroa

V-26. Wood figure of an ancestress

created by beating the inner bark fibers of a species of tree into a kind of felt, which they then painted freehand in geometric patterns or stamped with color (Plate V-22).

In the western island groups—Samoa and Tonga—craftsmanship was concentrated on the intricate surface decoration of wooden objects, especially clubs, in geometric patterns, a tradition we see, too, in the Cook and Austral Islands. In the figure of the great god Tangaroa (Plate V-23), from Rurutu in the Austral group, we see the god in the act of creating lesser gods and men, executed with a combined realistic and stylized treatment. The back of the figure is hollowed so that smaller images can be placed inside it to absorb divine power. In Ha'apai, of the Tongan group, some very beautiful small figures in walrus ivory and wood were produced, like the solid, well-formed little ivory female figure in Plate V-24.

In spite of frequent stylization, the human figure (by far the most frequent model) is usually recognizable in Polynesian art. It does not generally disintegrate or become merely a formal element in a pattern, such as we have seen in parts of Melanesia. Polynesian figures, like those in Plates V-25 and V-26, have a motionless quality of controlled force which suggests the eternal presence of the spirit which occupies them and with whose power they are charged. These two figures are the product of an authoritarian, ordered society. The carving is finer, the lines smoother and more simplified than we have seen in the figures of Melanesia. (It is interesting to note their abbreviated legs and feet.) These are ancestral figures, and the male represents a desiccated corpse, although the female, a flat form with only the head modeled in depth, does not.

Both these figures were found on Easter

V-27. Figures of ancestors, carved in volcanic tuffa

Island, one of the farthest outposts of Polynesian civilization and a riddle to historians. Discovered on Easter day of 1722, it stands in the barren isolation of the Pacific, two thousand miles from the coast of Chile to the east, and eleven hundred miles from Pitcairn, the nearest inhabited island to the west. The population of Easter Island could never have been more than five or six thousand souls. And yet it is covered with literally hundreds of enormous stone figures—huge heads and abbreviated bodies, usually surmounting burial platforms that fringe the island. The statues, from three to thirty-six feet in height, cut out of easily worked volcanic tuff, were quarried from a crater on the island. But how were these immense stone images (one seventy feet long was cut, although never moved, and others weighed up to fifty tons) hauled into place? And by whom? The population of the island would seem to have been too small to have created such gigantic stone monuments. Was it a sacred island to which pilgrims came across thousands of miles of open sea?

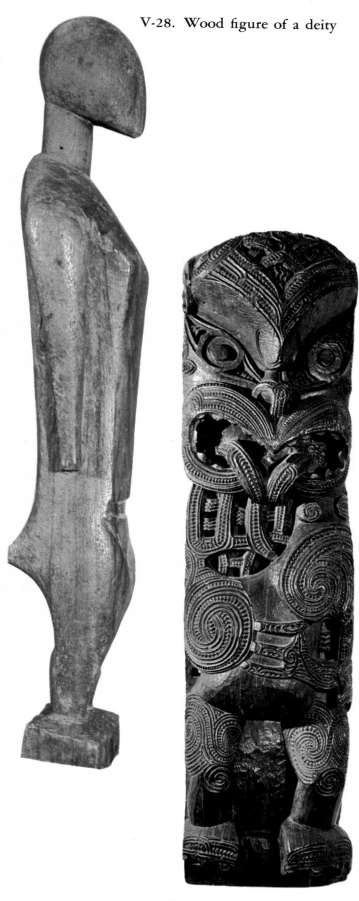

V-28. Wood figure of a deity

V-29. **Figure of an ancestor**

Again, in these strange figures with their large heads, long ears, and skimpy arms, we see the Polynesian tendency to reduce the human body to its bare essentials, a series of interesting planes and curves (Plate V-27). This same tendency was carried even further in the Polynesian colony of Nukuoro, far across the Pacific in the Carolines, a Micronesian group in the northwest. Here the face lacks even features (Plate V-28). Generally speaking, the islands of Micronesia are far less rich in art than those of Polynesia or Melanesia. This may be partly due to the extreme scarcity of trees in these islands, where even the sea vessels are sometimes made of small pieces of wood tightly joined together.

Maori art, the art of the Polynesian settlers of New Zealand, is in strong contrast to the simplified forms of Polynesian art which we have just been examining. The Polynesians who reached New Zealand entered a temperate climate with a totally strange flora and fauna—strange even to us. There were no mammals except bats to be found on land, although there were lizards, frogs, and many birds. The greatest single factor affecting their art was probably the abundance of fine wood, which apparently encouraged the multiplication of surface decoration and the development of a superb curvilinear style in which spirals are common, every inch of space is often decorated, and figures may be portrayed in violent and contorted movement. Maori gods were represented by insignificant-looking carved pegs which were set in the ground; the well-known figures represent ancestors and mythical creatures. The figure of an ancestor in Plate V-29 is such a work. Its swirling decoration in low relief, with deep perforations, is typical of Maori carving. So are the slanting, furious eyes, the protruding tongue, the snarling figure-eight-shaped mouth and three-fingered hand of this creature, part man and part beast.

Such figures were set up along the walls of the tribal meeting houses, which were lavishly ornamented with carved relief. Carving was tremendously important to the Maori. The chiefs themselves were sometimes carvers, and carved works were treasured. The acts of building and carving a house were accompanied by religious ceremonies, and at times even by human sacrifice.

Storehouses, canoe prows and sterns, and lidded boxes for storing valuables were among the many other types of wooden objects which were often beautifully carved. The Maori also found in New Zealand a material unique in Polynesia: nephrite, a green veined stone, a form of jade. Their well-developed stone technology enabled them to use this tough material for making not only excellent adze blades and chisels, but also the small neck ornaments, or amulets, called *hei-tiki* and other decorative objects. Such a hei-tiki is seen in Plate V-30. Like many, it suggests a human embryo, with staring inlaid eyes.

The Maori community of New Zealand is striving to keep its identity today, and to maintain the quality of its art. Unfortunately, this is not true of many of the other peoples of Oceania, whose visual arts are now almost extinct. Only in a few parts of Melanesia, especially in New Guinea, are pieces of high quality still made for native use. Elsewhere, as in Africa, carvings are made for sale, often in traditional style, but generally of poor workmanship.

What of the continent of Australia itself? Australia was a cultural backwater, largely cut off from contact with the outside world. The aborigines possess a material culture more simple than others in Oceania and very different. They live en-

V-30. Hei-tiki, carved in nephrite

tirely by hunting and collecting. This necessitates a wandering life in small bands, and material possessions must be light and portable.

Religion is the basis of nearly all Australian art. The aborigines believe that they are descended from mythical ancestors who lived in the remote past, the "dream time." These beings had the characteristics of both human beings and animals, which are also descended from them. To the aboriginal group the species sharing a common ancestor with them is their totem animal, which must not be killed or eaten, and the group increases the species by performing ceremonies that often include miming its actions.

Two important types of sacred objects, bull roarers and *churinga,* must not be seen by women or the uninitiated on pain of death. Bull roarers are made of wood, and are whirled on a string to make a moaning sound which is the "voice" of the totem. They bear patterns similar to those found on the churinga. These are slabs of wood or stone incised with designs which may seem to us simply abstract decoration—but they are much more. The symbols of Australian art take the place of written language, and the pattern we see in Plate V-31 has a hidden meaning. To the aborigines who can understand the meaning of the ocher shapes on this stone churinga, it tells of the wanderings of the totem animal and the places associated with it. Such a churinga serves as a bond between a man and his totemic ancestor.

The bark paintings of Arnhem Land also

V-31. Wooden churinga

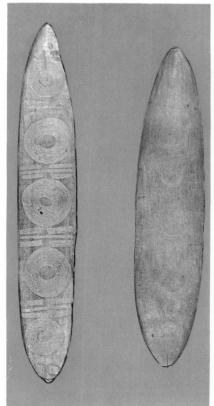

V-32. Painting on bark

depict mythical tales of totem creatures. Here we see the delicate drawing of the Australian aborigines, and again figures, some of them totally abstract and some semirealistic, the meaning of which can be read (Plate V-32).

Some of the most interesting products of Australian art cannot be preserved. These include painting and modeling on sand or smoothly compact earth. Moreover, many articles of daily use—weapons and utensils—are decorated with carved or painted totemic patterns, delicately drawn designs which give the object magical power. Among the most notable of these are shields (Plate V-33), boomerangs, and clubs.

Rock engravings and paintings are found in almost every part of Australia. Some are ancient and of unknown significance. Others are modern—they were still being painted as recently as 1936—and are known to be connected with the rites of initiation and with the bringing of rain and fertility. They vary in style from simple geometrical patterns and stenciled hands to realistic engraved outlines, silhouettes, and four-color paintings of men and animals. Naturally, the native art of Australia is disappearing with the disappearance of the bands of aborigines themselves.

The Australian aborigines have perhaps the simplest culture of any primitive people that we have seen, and yet like all men, everywhere, they share the urge to beautify the world around them, to make it more vivid—to summon up on a small surface a story, an illusion of life—in short, to create art and to thus contact the realm of the magical. In the words of Erwin Christensen, "In the case of the Australian aborigines, we have a people who wear no clothes, but paint their bodies; who build no houses, but paint on rock walls, slabs of

V-33. Painted and incised shield

stone, bark and the ground itself."[6] And so we see that the urge to create art is one of the bonds that unite all men, everywhere, at every period in their history.

[6]*Ibid.*, p. 312.

LIST OF ILLUSTRATIONS

II-31. Fragment of a mural. Teotihuacán culture. Classical period. Regional Museum, Teotihuacán.

II-32. Painted pottery mask. Teotihuacán culture. Classical period. National Museum of Anthropology, Mexico.

II-33. Stone funerary mask. Teotihuacán culture. Classical period. Musée de l'Homme, Paris.

II-34. Alabaster funeral mask. Teotihuacán culture. Classical period. Robert Woods Bliss Collection, Washington.

II-35. Funerary mask with turquoise mosaic inlay. Teotihuacán culture. Classical period. National Museum of Anthropology, Mexico.

II-36. View of the ceremonial center of Mount Albán. Zapotec culture. Classical period. Monte Albán.

II-37. One of a series of relief slabs known as "The Dancers." Zapotec culture. Formative period. Monte Albán.

II-38. Funerary urn with figure of a goddess. Zapotec culture. Classical period. National Museum of Anthropology, Mexico.

II-39. Funerary urn with figure of a seated dignitary. Zapotec culture. Classical period. Private collection, Mexico.

II-40. Funerary urn with figure of a goddess. Zapotec culture. Classical period. National Museum of Anthropology, Mexico.

II-41. Jade pectoral ornament in the form of a bat god. Zapotec culture. Classical period. National Museum of Anthropology, Mexico.

II-42. A. Jade mosaic mask.
B. Stucco head
Maya. Classical period. National Museum of Anthropology, Mexico.

II-43. Hieroglyphic writing engraved on stone. Maya. Classical period. Tabasco Museum, Villahermosa.

II-44. Kneeling worshiper before a serpent god, from a temple at Yaxchilán. Maya. Classical period. British Museum, London.

II-45. Detail of relief from the Temple of the Sun at Palenque. Maya. Classical period.

II-46. Limestone bust of the maize god, Copán, Honduras. Maya. Classical period. British Museum, London.

II-47. Stela P, Copán, Honduras. Maya. Classical period.

II-48. Painted pottery incense-burner. Maya. Classical period. National Museum of Anthropology, Mexico.

II-49. Jade plaque portraying a seated dignitary. Maya. Classical period. American Museum of Natural History, New York.

II-50. Kneeling pottery figurine, from the island of Jaina. Maya. Classical period. Private collection, Milan.

II-51. Pottery figurine of a seated ruler. Maya. Classical period. Robert Woods Bliss Collection, Washington.

II-52. Standing pottery figure. Maya. Classical period. Robert Woods Bliss Collection, Washington.

II-53. Pottery figure of a warrior carrying a shield and wearing a skull trophy. Maya. Classical period. Private collection, Mexico.

II-54. Cylindrical polychrome vase. Maya. Classical period. Nebaj, Guatemala. British Museum, London.

II-55. A battle scene. Fresco from the Temple of the Wall Paintings, Bonampak. Maya. Classical period. National Museum of Anthropology, Mexico.

II-56. False arch of the "Governor's Palace," Uxmal, Yucatán. Maya. Classical period, Puuc style.

II-57. Entrance to the Labná Palace, Yucatán. Maya. Classical period, Puuc style.

II-58. Temple of the Sun, Palenque. Maya. Classical period.

II-59. The Temple of the Inscriptions, Palenque. Maya. Classical period.

II-60. The Palace, Palenque. Maya. Classical period.

II-61. The K'odžp'op, Kabah, Yucatán. Maya. Classical period, Puuc style.

II-62. The "Governor's Palace," Uxmal, Yucatán. Maya. Classical period, Puuc style.

II-63. View of the quadrangle of "The Nunnery," Uxmal, Yucatán. Maya. Classical period, Puuc style.

II-64. The quadrangle of "The Nunnery," Uxmal, Yucatán. Maya. Classical period, Puuc style.

II-65. Courtyard for the ball game, Mount Albán, Oaxaca. Zapotec culture. Classical period.

II-66. The Chinkultic disc-marker for a ball court. Maya. Classical period. National Museum of Anthropology, Mexico.

II-67. Carved stone yoke. Vera Cruz culture. Classical period. American Museum of Natural History, New York.

II-68. A basalt axe, or hacha. Vera Cruz culture. Classical period. National Museum of Anthropology, Mexico.

II-69. Palmate stone in the form of a human head. Vera Cruz culture. Classical period. National Museum of Anthropology, Mexico.

II-70. Seated couple in pottery. Nayarit style. Private collection, Mexico.

II-71. Two seated figures in clay. Nayarit style. Museum of Primitive Art, New York.

II-72. Seated woman with plate, in clay. Jalisco style. Museum of Primitive Art, New York.

II-73. Thatched house with inhabitants. Nayarit style. Museum of Primitive Art, New York.

II-74. Pottery effigy of a Mexican hairless dog. Colima style. Private collection, Mexico.

II-75. Pyramid of Quetzalcoatl, Tula. Toltec. Post-Classical period.

II-76. Court of the Thousand Columns and Temple of the Warriors, Chichén Itzá. Maya-Toltec. Post-Classical period.

II-77. Pyramid called El Castillo, Chichén Itzá. Maya-Toltec. Post-Classical period.

II-78. Temple of the Warriors showing plumed-serpent columns, Chichén Itzá. Maya-Toltec. Post-Classical period.

II-79. Pillars in the form of warriors from the Temple of Quetzalcoatl, Tula. Toltec. Post-Classical period.

II-80. Rear view of the pillars of the Temple of Quetzalcoatl, Tula. Toltec. Post-Classical period.

II-81. Stone warrior. Toltec. Post-Classical period. National Museum of Anthropology, Mexico.

II-82. Stone figure from the Temple of the Warriors, Chichén Itzá. Maya-Toltec. Post-Classical period. National Museum of Anthropology, Mexico.

II-83. Chac-Mool figure, Chichén Itzá. Maya-Toltec. Post-Classical period. National Museum of Anthropology, Mexico.

II-84. Jaguar throne, Chichén Itzá. Maya-Toltec. Post-Classical period. National Museum of Anthropology, Mexico.

II-85. Relief detail from the facade of the Temple of Quetzalcoatl, Tula. Toltec. Post-Classical period.

II-86. Relief from wall of the great ball court, Chichén Itzá. Maya-Toltec. Post-Classical period.

II-87. Detail of relief from the ball court showing skulls, Chichén Itzá. Maya-Toltec. Post-Classical period.

II-88. Stela with relief representing a jaguar holding a human heart. Maya-Toltec. Post-Classical period. National Museum of Anthropology, Mexico.

II-89. The Tzompantli, Chichén Itzá. Maya-Toltec. Post-Classical period.

II-90. The Cenote of Sacrifice, Chichén Itzá. Maya-Toltec. Post-Classical period.

II-91. Gold figures dredged up from the Cenote of Sacrifice at Chichén Itzá, probably from Costa Rica. Post-Classical period. National Museum of Anthropology, Mexico.

II-92. The pyramid at Tenayuca. Aztec. Post-Classical period.

II-93. Stone figure of Coatlicue. Aztec. Post-Classical period. National Museum of Anthropology, Mexico.

II-94. Figure of Coatlicue. Aztec. Post-Classical period. National Museum of Anthropology, Mexico.

II-95. Stone figure of Quetzalcoatl. Aztec. Post-Classical period. National Museum of Anthropology, Mexico.

II-96. Statue of Ehecatl. Aztec. Post-Classical period. British Museum, London.

II-97. Seated figure of the god Xipe Totec. Aztec. Post-Classical period. Museum of Archaeology and History of the State of Mexico, Toluca.

II-98. A. Mask of Xipe Totec. Aztec. Post-Classical period. Museum of Ethnology, Vienna.

IV-29. Nimba bust. Baga. Musée de l'Homme, Paris.
IV-30. Drum with Nimba figures. Baga. Musée de l'Homme, Paris.
IV-31. Carved top of mask with hornbill. Baga. Musée de l'Homme, Paris.
IV-32. Soapstone statuette. Kissi. Musée de l'Homme, Paris.
IV-33. Anthropomorphic stone statue. Kissi. Musée de l'Homme, Paris.
IV-34. Nomoli soapstone figure. Sherbro. British Museum, London.
IV-35. Man's head in soapstone. Sherbro. Museum of Primitive Art, New York.
IV-36. Wooden mask. Dan. Musée de l'Homme, Paris.
IV-37. Two wooden masks. Kran. Musée de l'Homme, Paris.
IV-38. Wooden antelope mask. Guro. Musée de l'Homme, Paris.
IV-39. Wooden female figure. Baulé. Private collection, Milan.
IV-40. Wooden figure of a woman wearing bead ornaments. Baulé. Museum of Primitive Art, New York.
IV-41. Wooden mask. Baulé. Collection of Charles Ratton, Paris.
IV-42. Wooden mask. Baulé. Private collection, Milan.
IV-43. Gbekre, the monkey god. Baulé. Museum of Primitive Art, New York.
IV-44. Sculptured drum. Baulé. Musée de l'Homme, Paris.
IV-45. Mouse-oracle box. Baulé. Musée de l'Homme, Paris.
IV-46. Small golden mask. Baulé. Musée de l'Homme, Paris.
IV-47. Gold jewel. Baulé. Musée de l'Homme, Paris.
IV-48. A'kua'ba doll. Ashanti. Musée de l'Homme, Paris.
IV-49. Soul-washers' badges. Ashanti. British Museum, London.
IV-50. Elaborate gold bead from necklace. Ashanti. British Museum, London.
IV-51. Gelede mask. Yoruba. British Museum, London.
IV-52. Wooden mask. Yoruba. Brooklyn Museum, New York.
IV-53. Epa mask. Yoruba. Museum of Primitive Art, New York.
IV-54. Ivory horseman. Yoruba. British Museum, London.
IV-55. Woman suckling a child. Yoruba. Museum of Primitive Art, New York.
IV-56. Statuette of a twin. Yoruba. Musée de l'Homme, Paris.
IV-57. Bronze head of a king (oni). British Museum, London.
IV-58. Portrait head of a king. Ife. British Museum, London.
IV-59. Head of a king. Ife. British Museum, London.
IV-60. Bust in bronze. Ife. British Museum, London.
IV-61. Terra-cotta head. Ife. British Museum, London.
IV-62. Portrait head of a queen mother. Benin. British Museum, London.
IV-63. Bronze plaque. Benin. Nelson Gallery of Art, Kansas City.
IV-64. Oba riding in procession. Benin. British Museum, London.
IV-65. Head of an oba with tusk. Benin. Nelson Gallery of Art, Kansas City.
IV-66. Ivory scepter with captain on horseback. Benin. British Museum, London.
IV-67. Terra-cotta vase with seated woman. Bini. British Museum, London.
IV-68. Ancient head in terra cotta. Nok. Jos Museum, Nigeria.
IV-69. An ejiri, or "soul protector." Ijo. Museum of Primitive Art, New York.
IV-70. Wooden figure pounding grain. Ibo. British Museum, London.
IV-71. Painted wooden mask. Ibibio. British Museum, London.
IV-72. Skin-covered dance headdress. Ekoi. Musée de l'Homme, Paris.
IV-73. Seated man. Ekoi. British Museum, London.
IV-74. Wooden mask. Bamiléké. Museum of Ethnology, Vienna.
IV-75. Carved wooden doorframe. Bamiléké. Musée de l'Homme, Paris.
IV-76. King's throne. Bamiléké. British Museum, London.
IV-77. Figure of a man in wood. Fang. Musée de l'Homme, Paris.
IV-78. Head on elongated neck. Fang. Musée de l'Homme, Paris.
IV-79. Dance mask. Fang. British Museum, London.
IV-80. Dance mask in wood. Fang. British Museum, London.
IV-81. Heart-shaped dance mask. Bakwele. Private collection, Milan.
IV-82. Anthropomorphic figure. Bakota. Pigorini Museum, Rome.
IV-83. Reliquary figure. Bakota. Musée de l'Homme, Paris.
IV-84. Spirit mask. Balumbo. Museum of Primitive Art, New York.
IV-85. Ancestor statues in wood. Bakongo. Museum of Central Africa,
& 86. Tervuren.

IV-87. Soapstone carving of a man. Bakongo. Museum of Central Africa, Tervuren.
IV-88. Nail fetish. Bakongo. Pigorini Museum, Rome.
IV-89. Nail fetish. Bakongo. Museum of Central Africa, Tervuren.
IV-90. Painted dance mask with raffia beard. Bayaka. Brooklyn Museum, New York.
IV-91. Wooden figure of a drummer. Bayaka. Museum of Central Africa, Tervuren.
IV-92. Wooden initiation mask. Bapende. Museum of Central Africa, Tervuren.
IV-93. Figure of a woman and child. Bapende. Museum of Central Africa, Tervuren.
IV-94. Statue of Kwete Kata Mbula. Bakuba. Museum of Central Africa, Tervuren.
IV-95. Statue of Kwete Peshanga Kena. Bakuba. National Museum, Copenhagen.
IV-96. Dance mask. Bakuba. Museum of Central Africa, Tervuren.
IV-97. Woman and child. Bena Lulua. Museum of Central Africa, Tervuren.
IV-98. Figure of a chief. Bena Lulua. Museum of Central Africa, Tervuren.
IV-99. Figure of a girl. Bena Lulua. Museum of Central Africa, Tervuren.
IV-100. Fetish. Bena Lulua. Tropical Museum, Amsterdam.
IV-101. Wooden stool. Baluba. Museum of Primitive Art, New York.
IV-102. Headrest. Baluba. Museum of Central Africa, Tervuren.
IV-103. Wooden bowl. Baluba. Museum of Central Africa, Tervuren.
IV-104. Arrow holder. Baluba. Brooklyn Museum, New York.
IV-105. Dance mask. Basonge. Museum of Primitive Art, New York.
IV-106. Dance mask. Basonge. Museum of Central Africa, Tervuren.
IV-107. Fetish. Basonge. Museum of Central Africa, Tervuren.
IV-108. Seated man. Bajokwe. Private collection, Lasne, Belgium.
IV-109. Tobacco mortar. Bajokwe. Museum of Central Africa, Tervuren.
IV-110. Seat supported by caryatids. Bajokwe. Museum of Central Africa, Tervuren.
IV-111. Ivory mask. Balega. British Museum, London.
IV-112. Anthropomorphic figure in ivory. Balega. Museum of Central Africa, Tervuren.

THE ART OF AUSTRALIA AND OCEANIA

V-1. Map of Oceanic cultural areas.
V-2. Map of New Guinea.
V-3. Ceremonial stool. Melanesia. Sepik River, New Guinea. Museum of Anthropology, Basle.
V-4. Ancestor figure. Melanesia. Santa Cruz group. Museum of Primitive Art, New York.
V-5. Ancestor figure. Melanesia. West Irian, New Guinea. Museum of Anthropology, Basle.
V-6. Wood figure representing a spirit. Melanesia. Papuan Gulf, New Guinea. Museum of Primitive Art, New York.
V-7. Malanggan carving. Melanesia. New Ireland. Museum of Anthropology and Prehistory, Hamburg.
V-8. Figure from the supporting post of a chief's house. Melanesia. West Irian, New Guinea. Museum of Anthropology, Basle.
V-9. Upper portion of a central post, probably of a cult house. Melanesia. Sepik River, New Guinea. Museum of Anthropology, Basle.
V-10. Wood roof finial in the form of a duck. Melanesia. West Irian, New Guinea. Museum of Anthropology, Basle.
V-11. Wood rigging block of a canoe. Melanesia. Massim district, New Guinea. Pigorini Museum, Rome.
V-12. Carved wood ornament from the prow of a canoe. Melanesia. Admiralty Islands. Museum of Anthropology and Prehistory, Hamburg.
V-13. Blade of a paddle. Melanesia. Solomon Islands. Pigorini Museum, Rome.
V-14. Shield. Melanesia. West Irian, New Guinea. Museum of Anthropology, Basle.

V-15. Painting on sheets of sago palm-leaf sheaths. Melanesia. Sepik River, New Guinea. Museum of Anthropology, Basle.

V-16. Mask representing the founder of a clan. Melanesia. Sepik River, New Guinea. Museum of Anthropology, Basle.

V-17. Mask of painted barkcloth. Melanesia. New Britain. Museum of Anthropology, Basle.

V-18. Mask of tree-fern wood. Melanesia. New Hebrides. Museum of Anthropology, Basle.

V-19. Mask of painted wood. Melanesia. Sepik River, New Guinea. National Museum, Copenhagen.

V-20. Wood figure of a deity. Polynesia. Hawaii. Bishop Museum, Honolulu.

V-21. Head of the war god Kukailimoku. Polynesia. Hawaii. Bishop Museum, Honolulu.

V-22. Barkcloth. Polynesia. Hawaii. Private collection, Milan.

V-23. Figure of the great god Tangaroa. Polynesia. Austral Islands. British Museum, London.

V-24. Ivory female figure. Polynesia. Tonga Islands. Museum of Primitive Art, New York.

V-25. Wood figure of an ancestor. Polynesia. Easter Island. Museum of Man, Paris.

V-26. Wood figure of an ancestress. Polynesia. Easter Island. Museum of Primitive Art, New York.

V-27. Figures of ancestors, carved in volcanic tuffa. Polynesia. Easter Island.

V-28. Wood figure of a deity. Micronesia. Nukuoro, Caroline Islands. Museum of Anthropology and Prehistory, Hamburg.

V-29. Figure of an ancestor. Polynesia. New Zealand. Museum of Primitive Art, New York.

V-30. Hei-tiki, carved in nephrite. Polynesia. New Zealand. British Museum, London.

V-31. Wooden churinga. Australia. Museum of Man, Paris.

V-32. Painting on bark. Australia. Arnhem Land. State Museum of Folk Art, Frankfort.

V-33. Painted and incised shield. Australia. Victoria. Museum of Man, Paris.

INDEX